A Catalogue of the Works of Ralph Shapey

Ralph Shapey (photo by Jim Wright).

A CATALOGUE OF THE WORKS OF RALPH SHAPEY

By Patrick Finley

DIMENSION & DIVERSITY No.1
Mark DeVoto, General Editor

PENDRAGON PRESS
STUYVESANT, NY

Other titles in the series **Dimension and Diversity: Studies in Twentieth-Century Music**
No. 2 *Brecht and Music: A Documentation* by Ronald K. Shull and
　　Joachim Lucchesi (in press) ISBN 0-945193-18-1

Library of Congress Cataloging-in-Publication Data

Finley, Patrick D. (Patrick Daniel)
　　A catalogue of the works of Ralph Shapey / by Patrick D. Finley.
　　　p.　cm. — (Dimension and diversity)
　　Includes bibliographical references and discography.
　　ISBN 0-945193-89-0
　　1. Shapey, Ralph, 1921—Bibliography. I. Title. II. Series.
　　ML134.S445F56　1997
　　016.78'092—dc20　　　　　　　　　　　　　　96-35214
　　　　　　　　　　　　　　　　　　　　　　　　　CIP
　　　　　　　　　　　　　　　　　　　　　　　　　MN

Copyright 1997 Pendragon Press

CONTENTS

Acknowledgments	vi
Introduction	vii
The Biography	1
The Catalogue	19
Shapey's Compositional Method	63
The Mother Lode	65
Analyses	69
Appendix A: Scores for Analyses	
Evocation No. 3	75
Krosnick Soli	78
Psalm I for Soprano Oboe and Piano	79
Master of the Universe	80
Theme Plus Ten	84
Concertante No. II for Alto Saxophone and Fourteen Players	87
Appendix B: Works Arranged by Medium/Instrumental Forces	93
Appendix C: Discography	99
Bibliography	105

ACKNOWLEDGMENTS

First of all, I would like to thank Professor Bruce Saylor for making me a better writer, and Dr. Marilyn Stearns, Drs. Frank and Susan Carden, and Robert Cohen for their careful editing. Also, thanks to Tom Broido at Presser Publishers for giving me access to their files. Especially, thanks to Ralph Shapey for his hours given to going through his manuscripts to fill the gaps in the catalogue, for allowing me to interrupt his busy schedule with numerous, lengthy phone calls concerning the analyses, and for fixing it so that I'll never compose the same way again. Last, but not least, I would like to thank my wife Christine and my children Morgan and Leslie. Without their years of patience and support, this project would never have been completed.

INTRODUCTION

The purpose of this catalogue is to list the works of the composer Ralph Shapey, with additional information that might serve—among others—students, performers, and librarians.

The catalogue information herein was gathered primarily from Presser Publications in Bryn Mawr, PA, where several files of program notes, clippings of reviews, and final copies of Shapey's works are kept. In addition, information was gathered from the holdings of the New York Public Library and Shapey's private collection.

The listing is as comprehensive as possible, inclusive even of certain early works withdrawn from publication at the request of the composer. Certain entries contain information sent to me by Shapey. Those items where Shapey personally supplies the information are followed by his initials in parentheses: *(r.s.)*. Where there is no information available in a given category, that category has been eliminated from the entry. Furthermore, it should be added that the listing is comprehensive as of November, 1996. Ralph Shapey is still very active as a composer, and at a rate which will probably render this project incomplete by the end of the year.

ENTRIES

Each entry is numbered chronologically and includes eleven categories of information. Certain categories require amplification.

Movements

For the sake of clarity and consistency, the movements in the catalogue are preceded by roman numerals and separated by a semicolon. However, it should be noted that few of the composer's final copies and few concert programs use roman numerals in listing the movements.

Duration

The Duration of each entry is given at the end of the listing of movements. Unless otherwise stated, the duration is that written on the score.

Medium

Standard abbreviations for instrumental forces are used. That is, the first four numerals (e.g. 2.2.2.2.) represent the woodwinds (flute, oboe, clarinet, bassoon). The second four numerals represent the brass (french horn, trumpet, trombone, tuba). Doublings are not indicated. Other instruments (saxophone, piano, etc.) are listed individually with conventional abbreviations. The normal complement of strings is listed as "str."

Date

Where a single date is given, it refers to the date of completion. Where two dates are given, the first is the date Shapey began the work and the second is the date of completion. In some cases only the year of composition could be ascertained. The place where the work was begun and completed is given where known.

Final Copy

This category includes the length in pages and the material of the final copy (e.g., "ink on tissue"). All of the scores examined are final copies in the possession of Presser Publishers. Shapey tells us that they were all copied in his own hand until about 1992 when he began using a copyist. Those scores not in Shapey's hand will be indicated in this category by the designation "copyist." Where the score was unavailable, the length in measures is given, taken from the parts.

The composer's manuscripts (i.e., sketches and drafts) are in the composer's possession in Chicago. Shapey has agreed to bequeath his working copies to the Regenstein Library of the University of Chicago.

Publication

All of the works of Shapey are published by Theodore Presser. Those works that have Presser catalogue numbers have those numbers listed in this category. There are three types of publication:

> *Published*—means the "authorized reproduction of the composer's manuscript" (i.e., the composer's final copy),[1] or a work written out by a copyist.
>
> *Published—special order*—means that the authorized reproduction is not bound, but will be copied, bound, and sold by request.
>
> *Published (Engr.)*—means that the work has been engraved.

Rental—means that the authorized reproduction is available for rental.

Dedication

In most cases, the dedication is quoted directly from the composer's final copy. Occasionally, the program notes were the source of this information.

First Performance

This category lists the date, location, and performers, when known.

Reviews and Articles

Reviews and articles are listed in chronological order. Reviews of premieres are preceded by (P).

Notes

This category supplies the reader with supplemental information, e.g., annotations in the autograph score, literary sources of texts of vocal works, commissions, the composer's comments.

---

[1] Presser's description of the composer's final copy. This description is on several of Shapey's published works.

THE BIOGRAPHY

THE BIOGRAPHY

Ralph Shapey was born March 12, 1921, in Philadelphia, where he lived with his mother, father, and younger brother until he was graduated from high school. Shapey never knew nor does he recall being told anything about his grandparents. His father, who immigrated from Russia in 1905, was a cabinet maker. When he first arrived in America he worked for an antique shop. After the Depression he worked for the Philco Radio Corporation, and was assigned to hand-crafting the cabinets for a very expensive line of units that combined the newfangled television with a radio and turntable. Shapey's mother worked at various department stores in Philadelphia so that the family could live more comfortably in the years just after the Depression. Shapey's younger brother Ronald Sidney Shapey became a violinist with the Cincinnati Orchestra; he died in 1991 of a massive heart attack.

An event that was to influence Shapey for the rest of his life took place shortly after his birth. His father told him the story many times. Ralph had contracted double pneumonia. Medical advances being what they were in the 1920's, the doctor held out little hope. "The only thing I can suggest," he said to Ralph's parents, "is to have another baby."

Ralph's father found the advice unacceptable. He began to reason: "If Ralph's problem is the fluid in his lungs, then all we have to do is to get the fluid out and he might live." So Shapey's father grabbed his naked baby by the ankles, held him up, and began to smack him on his back and backside over and over. The baby screamed hysterically. He also began coughing up mucus. After a little while Ralph's father stopped hitting him and laid him in his crib, where he cried for a bit more and then fell asleep. When the baby awoke, his condition had improved. Shapey calls this story "The Shapey Mythology." He adds: "Because of this incident, all my life I have felt that an angel of life sits on my one shoulder, and an angel of death sits on the other."

Shapey continued to have respiratory troubles all his life. As a child, whenever he came down with a cold, he was out of school for two to four weeks with bronchitis, "and I always felt like I was spending more time in a doctor's office than in school."

Shapey was educated in Philadelphia's public school system. He recalls: "I did very well in subjects I liked, and not too well at all in subjects I disliked, or in classes taught by teachers who were stupid. And a lot of them were stupid." Shapey argued frequently in class with his teachers. He was graduated in 1939 with satisfactory but undistinguished grades. Shapey's graduation from high school marked the end of his last formal education.

When he was five years old, Shapey broke his right wrist in an accident. He broke the same wrist again shortly after, and a third time at age seven, when a friend yanked him hard out of the path of a runaway horse and wagon ("Again," Shapey says, "my brush with death!"). In spite of this third fracture, he began to study the violin that same year. Two years later, he gave his first recital. He was declared a child prodigy by his teachers, and this recital marked the beginning of a career in music that would take him all over the world.

When he turned sixteen, Shapey auditioned for Emmanuel Zetlin who resided in New York City, and taught at the Queen Street Settlement music school in Philadelphia. Zetlin, a soloist who at one time had been an assistant to Carl Flesh at the Curtis Institute, was a short, thin, reserved man with inescapable steel-blue eyes. He always addressed everyone as *Mr., Miss,* or *Mrs.,* never by their first names. "At my audition, after listening to my performance of the Beethoven Violin Concerto, Zetlin replied 'My boy, you are a diamond that needs polishing.'"

Lessons with Emmanuel Zetlin were more like recitals. "He would sit curled up in a wicker chair," recalls Shapey. "During one's lesson, if he stayed curled up, you packed up your violin and left. If he liked it, he'd uncurl and sing, coach, and sometimes accompany. (He was an excellent pianist.) At one lesson I played a Bach solo sonata, the Sibelius Violin Concerto, and a Wieniawski solo etude. He said to me: 'very nice, very nice. Now would you mind playing the C♯ minor scale in tenths?'... I packed up and left. He didn't know me very well yet, but he was about to get to know me a little better. At the next lesson, I started by playing the C♯ minor scale in tenths. When I finished, Zetlin did something he seldom did...he laughed."

It was common practice at the school for Zetlin's other students to stand outside the door and listen as their colleagues played. At one lesson, Ralph played a work, and Mr. Zetlin uncurled himself from his wicker chair. He rose and started talking to Shapey. He finished the lesson saying, "Mr. Shapey, please remember: the deeper the hurt, the greater the joy."

When Ralph stepped outside he was surrounded by a small group of students who excitedly asked him about the long silence. Ralph told his friends about Zetlin's remarks. "They were all shocked and decided that Zetlin must have flipped out of his mind, because it was the only time in anyone's memory that he spoke on a personal level to any student." In 1942 Shapey finished his studies with Zetlin. By that time Shapey had played all of the concerto literature for the violin.

In 1938 Shapey had begun classroom music studies with Stefan Wolpe. Shapey had been studying theory, harmony, and counterpoint "with various teachers" before that, but he recalls his beginning studies with Wolpe particularly. "One day in class, Stefan was playing an exercise for us at the piano and I blurted out 'why don't you tune that damn thing!'" Ralph admits that he does not have perfect pitch, but he could hear that the piano was slightly out of tune. When Stefan played the instrument for a while longer he realized that Ralph had heard instantly what he himself had not noticed. "After class he took me aside and asked if I was doing any composing. When I said that I was doing a little, he asked to see my work, and my compositional studies with Stefan began, although at this point I was still merely dabbling in it."

It took a bit of pleading with his parents, but in his junior year Shapey transferred to Mastbaum Vocational High School, a post-graduate high school with music courses, rated second only to the Curtis Institute. It was an honor to have been accepted. Nonetheless, Shapey recalls that he considered most of his studies in music at the school to be routine. "But there was one teacher who was very smart; at least, he was smart in how he handled me."

This was Mr. Meier Levin, Shapey's harmony teacher at Mastbaum. One day Levin kept Shapey after class to ask why he seemed so disinterested in the course work. "I don't like the class," Ralph explained, "because I'm not interested in the way traditional harmony sounds." Mr. Levin said to him, "Then I want you to complete the entire exercise book on harmony for me. But I want you to do it twice." Producing a second book for Shapey, he went on: "Fill out the first book the way I want you to, the way the textbooks want you to. Then fill out the second the way you hear harmony and melody."

"I went to work at once," recalls Ralph. "The first book I filled out by copying traditional harmonies from the text, and supplying the appropriate traditional-type melodies where I was supposed to, as fast as I could put down the notes. I practically did the thing blindfolded.

"But the second book! Now that was the one I was interested in. I filled out each exercise my way. And keep in mind, at this time I didn't care for modern music. I considered Stravinsky's early works masterpieces, but his neoclassical and twelve-tone stuff as well as the works of Schoenberg and those other guys I considered to be garbage. Nonetheless, everything in that second book was harmony as I heard it in my mind, and all the melodies were asymmetrical."

When Mr. Levin saw the book, he asked Shapey, "Where did you come up with all of these ideas?" Shapey replied, "I don't know, but that's how I hear music." On every one of the pages, Shapey's teacher wrote "A for audacity." In looking back on that book, Shapey now realizes that many themes used in his later works came from that little exercise book, which, unfortunately, Shapey believes is lost.

Ralph was now sixteen years old. That year, in Philadelphia, he attended the world premiere of Schoenberg's Violin Concerto. The work changed his attitude toward modern music completely: "I was enthralled, and I was utterly taken by the magnificence of it that music for the first time could speak on the level that I heard in my mind."[1] Little did Shapey dream that one day he would become one of the great spokesmen of this new language.

That same year, Shapey was selected Youth Conductor of the Philadelphia Youth Orchestra. Less than one year later, he was named the assistant conductor. Shapey's prodigal talents did not delight everyone. The post was an uncommon one for a sixteen-year-old, and when the Director of the Settlement Music School was informed about Shapey's appointment, he attempted to have Ralph ejected from the school. "I think he was jealous," remarked Shapey. "At any rate, Wolpe and Zetlin went to work on him. They told him he had some nerve trying to throw me out. They also told him that he should be honored that I am a student at the school, and that he should be proud of me. When they were finished with him, the letter requesting my dismissal was torn up. I stayed on, and we did some great concerts. The newspapers wrote rave reviews about the orchestra and my conducting."

For many young musicians in Philadelphia in those days, the Queen Street Settlement was the entry point into the Curtis Institute. Many of the students who studied in the former passed auditions into the latter. And from Curtis, many of those who played orchestral instruments made their way into the Philadelphia Orchestra, or went on to become members of the world's leading orchestras.

The list of students who played under Ralph's baton in those days is impressive. Most joined the Philadelphia Orchestra. Players such as violinist Veda Reynolds, first clarinetist Anthony Gigliotti, and Frances (cellist) and Joseph (violist) dePasquale. Violinist Jake Krachmalnick became concertmaster. Then there were those who, like Ralph Gomberg—who became first oboe with the Boston Symphony—disseminated throughout

---

[1] From an interview with Easley Blackwood, in the *Chicago Daily News,* Sept. 25, 1965.

the United States to various orchestras. Some wound up in Hollywood as studio musicians.

Although he had been studying composition with Wolpe, Shapey focused on working and studying as a violinist and conductor. His decision to become a composer was quite sudden. "I'll never forget it," he says. "Having conducted the previous Youth Symphony Concert, I was exempt from conducting or playing violin in the next one, what with conducting being so strenuous. Anyway, I was at home enjoying the evening off when I got a call from the manager: "Our conductor just copped out," he said, "you have to conduct the next concert. Rehearsal is tomorrow morning and the concert in the evening."

Shapey replied frantically: "Tomorrow? I don't even know what's on the program!" The manager read the program to him over the phone, and Ralph went to work. He stayed awake all night studying the scores, conducted the morning rehearsal, went home for a nap, and showed up for the concert that evening.

"At the concert, while I was conducting Beethoven's Eighth Symphony, everything was going fine," recalls Shapey. "Suddenly, during the fourth movement, there was a moment when my hand faltered—just for a few seconds. At that moment the thought flashed through my mind: 'Who do you think you are, conducting a great work like this? Do you think, just because you can wave your arms around better than somebody else, that you have the right to be up here conducting Beethoven? For you to be able to conduct, you have to be able to compose... really compose.' My mind snapped back to the music and we finished the concert. After that night I began my serious studies at composition."

In 1942, Shapey won the Philadelphia Finds Competition, which entitled him to conduct the Philadelphia Orchestra in one of its regular concerts at the Robin Hood Dell. But "then came that famous little argument over in Europe," Ralph says with a sigh. "I was declared fit for combat duty by virtue of having two arms, two legs, and one head, and was drafted into the army." Shapey petitioned his local draft board for an extension on his date, explaining that he had just won a prestigious competition, and was committed to conduct the Philadelphia Orchestra. The Draft Board would not relent, and Shapey was ordered to Alabama for basic training. Shapey used to tell people that he had no idea why the draft board denied his request for an extension on his date to report to active duty. "But I did know. One of the members of the draft board was the friend of one of the contestants in the competition. His friend lost and that fellow didn't give a damn about me and saw to it that I was shipped out."

However, Ralph had no intention of allowing the Army to deprive him of the most important opportunity he had yet been given. Very soon after reporting for basic training, Shapey went straight to his 1st sergeant and requested an emergency furlough. The sergeant explained that recruits are not permitted to have furloughs until they have completed basic training. "Besides," the sergeant said, "what could possibly be so important that you have to have a furlough?"

"I'm scheduled to conduct the Philadelphia Orchestra," Shapey replied. The stunned sergeant took Private Shapey straight to the Colonel's office. Shapey explained to the Colonel, and showed him the contract for his conducting debut with the Philadelphia Orchestra. The Colonel replied, "The 'Philadelphia' Philadelphia Orchestra?" and got on the phone instantly. "And you see," Ralph explained, "they had to let me go because my obligation with the Philadelphia Orchestra was agreed upon prior to my draft notice. I conducted on April 29, 1942. It was a huge success, and the papers did another article on me."[2]

After the war ended, Shapey moved to New York to resume his studies with Zetlin and Wolpe who, like Zetlin, lived in New York and taught in Philadelphia. But first he went to Louis Persinger (Yehudi Menuhin's teacher) to audition. After reading a letter of introduction written for Shapey by a friend of Persinger's, Persinger then asked Shapey if there was anything in particular about his playing that presently concerned him. "Everything," said Ralph. "My left hand is lousy, my bowing arm is lousy, my technique is lousy. . . everything is lousy."

Persinger asked what Ralph would like to play. Ralph told him that during his years of study under Zetlin he used the Sibelius Violin Concerto as his audition piece. Like Zetlin, Persinger was also an accomplished pianist. So he went to the piano, "and the two of us ripped into the Sibelius. Then somewhere into the second movement Persinger stopped playing and looked at me. 'How long did you say it's been since you've done any serious practicing?' he asked. 'Three years,' I said. And he shot back: 'Well, I've got news for you, young man. There is nothing wrong with your left hand, your bowing arm, or your technique. All you need is to practice, so go home and practice.'"

Ralph left the studio. A short time later he decided to resume his studies with Zetlin. Shapey settled in New York, where he would live until 1964.

In the early 1950's Shapey had landed a job in New York's Third Street Settlement Music School teaching violin, theory, harmony, and some composition, with an annual salary of about $2,500. He spent his evenings composing and conducting. "You have to understand New York in the early fifties," says Shapey. "There was almost nothing going on in the way of modern music, and what little there was, I was doing most of it. If I hadn't conducted Stefan Wolpe's music, it would never have been heard."

As one of the few conductors capable of handling modern music, Shapey was frequently on call—often without pay and on short notice—to serve as conductor, sometimes sight-reading the scores during rehearsals.

In 1952, Shapey entered the George Gershwin competition which was organized by Dimitri Mitropoulos, who was then director of both the NY Philharmonic and the NY Philharmonic Chamber Group. Mitropoulos saw to it that the latter frequently featured contemporary works. First prize went to a composer "whose last name was Travis, and who seems to have disappeared," says Ralph, sardonically. Shapey's Fantasy for Symphony Orchestra placed second. But Mitropoulos made it known to everyone—including the press—that the only reason Shapey's piece did not place first was that it was too difficult and would require too many rehearsals to perform it well, which Shapey now says is "a lot of BS."[3]

"Actually, I was in the auditorium with several friends and my students. Rumor has it that I mounted the stage and podium and pushed Dimitri aside to conduct, which is a blatant lie. It later turned out that Dimitri had pre-planned the cancellation because of the supposed difficulties both for him and the orchestra.

"History tells us that Beethoven rehearsed his first symphony for one entire year before daring to perform it publicly, and he was called crazy. The orchestra under Dimitri did only early

---

[2] See Appendix, p. 189.

[3] Mr. Shapey can afford to think this way. He is well-known for his ability to "teach" an orchestra how to play just about anything.

twentieth century composers: Schoenberg, Webern, Berg (complaining all the way)—hardly any mid-twentieth century works demanding extended ranges, glissandi, or any kind of different handling of their instrumental playing. The unfortunate truth is, I believe that Dimitri could have done the piece but was intimidated by the players. Despite this situation Dimitri and I remained friends, and years later Paul Fromm told me that Dimitri once said to him 'watch over Shapey; he's a genius.'[4] It was one of many incidents in which great men would befriend Ralph out of respect for his talents.

Also in 1952 Shapey married Sylvia Goldberg, a composition student of his as well as a gifted pianist and artist. Ralph admired her talents. He especially liked her pen-and-ink drawings. In fact, she designed some of the covers for his music. When Shapey had composed his Cantata in 1951, Sylvia had provided the text.

In the spring of 1953, Shapey decided that he should have a publisher. He visited the Peters Company in New York, and the president greeted him enthusiastically. "Yes, yes!" he said, "Of course I know you, Mr. Shapey! I have followed your career with great interest!" And the two of them sat down in the president's office. The president went through several pages of Shapey's music, staring intently at certain passages, and nodding approvingly from time to time. At length he looked up and said "Well, Ralph, there's no doubt about it: you're a genius. But to tell you the truth, we don't have time for geniuses these days."

"Without speaking, I stood up, scooped my music up from his desk and put it under my arm. I went to the door, turned back to him, said 'Fuck you,' and walked out. In the autumn of 1953, I won the Frank Huntington Bebe award, and Sylvia and I traveled to Europe for the first time. When I went to London, I visited Boosey and Hawkes with the same intention. The people at that office bowed and scraped as I walked by. It was incredible. I'd never been treated with so much reverence! Then, in his office, after looking through my manuscripts, the president said I'd be publishable when I was dead and buried. I gave him the same reply I'd given that gentleman at Peters."

It wasn't until 1977 that the Presser Company in Pennsylvania agreed to publish Shapey's music. To Ralph's dismay, this meant photocopying his final drafts in ink (some in pencil), putting a cover on them, and offering them for sale or rent. His first engraved work was *Twenty-One Variations for Piano,* in 1978. Gradually, other works were engraved as well. (See catalogue under "Final Copy.")

The remainder of Shapey's trip to Europe was basically pleasant. While in London, he met conductor Walter Goehr and his son "Sandy" (Alexander). One day Sandy showed Shapey one of his own compositions, saying: "Would you look this over for me? I asked my father to, but he says it's too modern, and he doesn't understand this kind of music." Ralph began going over the score. After a few moments he looked up and said: "You sure do like the Schoenberg *Hanging Gardens,* don't you?"

"My God," Sandy said. "You can see it?"

"See it?" replied Ralph, "It's all over the piece. And so what? You modeled your work after a good composer." From that time on, both Goehrs became close friends of Shapey.

On the wall of his apartment, Shapey has pictures of himself "with many of the great names in classical music: Louis Krasner, the Juilliard Quartet, Dallapiccola, Varese, Sessions, you name it; my rogue's gallery. And, as with the Goehrs, the

---

[4]Letter from Ralph Shapey, August, 1996.

basis of our friendship—one that I am proud of—was that of mutual admiration. When Dallapiccola came to New York I did a concert of his music and he was ecstatic over the performance. I know because my friend Henry Weinberg told me how pleased Dallapiccola was, and even Dallapiccola's wife told me. The same goes for Varese and many, many others."

From London Shapey went to Italy. There he had the opportunity to show his current work—his Concerto for Clarinet and Chamber Group—to Dimitri Mitropoulos, who was there conducting *The Girl of the Golden West*. Mitropoulos looked it over and said: "All right, Ralph. Okay. We're going to do this on one of the NY Philharmonic Chamber Concerts. Stanley Drucker (first clarinetist with the NY Philharmonic) will be the soloist. You conduct the rehearsals, and I'll do the concert." Shapey returned to the U. S., and some months later, was walking down 56th Street when he was startled by a hard slap on the back from behind. It was Dimitri Mitropoulos, who beamed at him and said, "I've changed my mind. You can conduct the performance as well. That's it."

"Fine," Ralph said.

"But you know at the end, that high B- natural?"

"Yeah," Ralph said, "I know it. C-sharp written pitch; the last note in the piece."

"Yes, that one," replied Mitropoulos. "Well, it can't be done."

"Oh, hell, Dimitri, it can too be done. Stanley can do it."

Dimitri Mitropoulos thought for a moment, then said, "Tell you what. The Philharmonic is rehearsing tomorrow. Drop by and bring the score. Drucker will be there. We'll let *him* settle it."

Shapey agreed, and the next morning he went to the rehearsal. The orchestra members were seated on the stage, busy with tuning, practicing various passages, and chatting, when Mitropoulos spotted Drucker. Mitropoulos and Shapey both stepped up to the podium, and Mitropoulos called Drucker over and showed him the place in Shapey's score with the high B. "Can you play that on a B-flat clarinet?" Mitropoulos asked. Without a word, Stanley Drucker went back to his seat, took his clarinet out of its case, wet a reed in his mouth, fastened it to his clarinet, and without even warming up, played a perfect high B. Mitropoulos threw up his hands in exasperation. Shapey still laughs hard when he tells this story. Rehearsals began soon after, and the work was performed on Sunday, March 20, 1955, at the YM-YWHA on 92nd Street in New York.

Later that year, Mitropoulos commissioned an orchestral work for the NY Philharmonic from Shapey which became his *Challenge–the Family of Man*. The commission consisted of Dimitri paying for the copying of the parts and two tickets to the performance for Shapey. At one point, Mitropoulos called Shapey to his penthouse apartment in the plush Great Northern Hotel to discuss the piece. Dimitri informed Ralph that he would like to leave out one entire section "because it upsets my equilibrium due to your asymmetrical rhythms."

"A forest is symmetrical," Dimitri pointed out pedantically.

"No, it isn't!" replied Ralph. "The forest totality is symmetrical, but it is made up of asymmetrical designs. The bark is thicker on the North side of the tree, and leaves are more abundant on the South side."

"We humans are symmetrical," Mitropoulos said.

"Also untrue. If one draws a line down our middle each side of our face is slightly different, each nostril, each eye...."

Mitropoulos threw up his hands in dismay.

Ralph recalls: "At the first rehearsal it became obvious that Mitropoulos was unable to conduct the work. The players refused to play, complaining about the glissandi (which are commonplace today), and the rhythms, which didn't fit into any standard umpah-umpah, etc. Dimitri again complained that the work was too difficult for the orchestra, and too difficult for him. Nor would he allow me to take over, despite his having seen me conduct.

"Dimitri chose to cancel the performance. The story put out was that the parts were not ready; this was in spite of the fact that the entire music world knew the truth. My phone didn't stop ringing for three days, with calls from friends and foes alike to commiserate with me. The episode made me famous, although the NY Philharmonic never attempted a work of mine again."

Meanwhile, Ralph's marriage was not going well. He and Sylvia agreed to a divorce in 1957.

Through all of this, Ralph had continued to perform on the violin, mostly on short-notice freelance jobs. But his busy schedule as conductor and composer was taking its toll on his technique. Gradually his work as conductor and composer would replace his work as violinist completely. As Shapey tells it: "I continued to take playing jobs, but I had to drop everything for a week or two and practice my tail off to get in shape. Misha Elman once said, 'If I don't practice for one day, I know it. If I don't practice for two days, the audience knows it, and if I don't practice for three days, the whole world knows it.' Anyway, one of my first jobs out of the army was with Adolf Busch and his chamber players. We were touring the United States by bus. Many times Adolf and I sat together in the front (when his student, the Naumberg Award-winner Francis Magnus, wasn't sitting with him), and one evening Adolf said to me: 'Ralph, you're a soloist. If you'll study with me full time, I guarantee you a Naumberg award.' I hesitated a bit, then agreed to take one lesson with him. At the end of it, I decided that I was kidding myself. I knew what I wanted to do.

"My last job as a violinist was in the early fifties in a recording studio with the Juilliard Quartet, in a piece written for three violins, viola, and cello. As I always did for these jobs, I dropped everything and went back to practicing. I was practicing six hours a day to get my muscles back into condition, and it was tough. My left arm hurt constantly. We recorded the work, and I went home and thought, 'Ralph, you have to make a decision. That piece wasn't that hard. What are you going to do? You can't do it all!' I decided to give up the violin completely. I continued to teach violin, but my days as a violinist were over."

During the summers from 1956 to 1959, Shapey worked and lived at the MacDowell Colony. There, in 1957, he met Vera Klement, already a well-known painter. Each respected the other's talents, and respect blossomed into romance. When they returned to New York in October 1957, they were married. At the colony, Shapey began his fifth String Quartet, which he completed in New York. Shapey dedicated it to his new wife, who supplied him with the text (as his first wife, Sylvia, had done for the Cantata).

Shortly after their return to the MacDowell Colony in 1959, Vera discovered she was pregnant, and in 1960 their son Max was born. He was to be Ralph's only child. Shapey's marriage to Vera would last another sixteen years, parting on good terms.

Saturday, May 13, 1962, emerged as one of the most thrilling nights in Shapey's life. In 1960, he had received his first commission from the Fromm Foundation. A concert of Fromm-commissioned works was arranged in New York, and on that Saturday night, Shapey's new work, *Dimensions,* premiered, along with works by Wolpe, Krenek, and Berger. That evening, backstage, one of the players approached Shapey, saying: "Ralph, they're all out there. Take a machine gun with you and you'll get them all."

Ralph looked out into the audience. "The guy was right," he recalls: "Composers and conductors from as far as Boston—Leinsdorf, Copland, the manager of the Boston Symphony, Babbitt, Varese, Carter (the party afterward was at Carter's apartment on 10th Street)—were there. What's more, Stefan and I had become close friends with several of the abstract expressionists, and *they* were there: Jack Tworkove, Harold Rosenburg, Dore Ashton (who called Shapey's *Incantations* an abstract expressionist work)—even De Kooning! The audience was loaded, and the concert was a tremendous success." Subsequently, Paul Fromm commissioned two more works from Shapey, which became his *Songs of Ecstasy* (1969), and his seventh *String Quartet* (1972).

By 1962 Ralph had composed over forty works, and had been reviewed in major newspapers throughout the country. He was being labeled everything from a phony to a prophet. He continued to receive commissions, and it seemed that wherever he went he was sought out as a conductor, and in the process would befriend one great artist or another. When Ralph conducted the London Symphonietta in his *Rituals* for symphony orchestra (for the CRI) recording and the Symphonietta needed to expand its members for the performance, many members of the London Symphony who had played under Shapey's baton previously in his *Invocation—Concerto for Violin and Orchestra* requested that they be permitted to work with him again.

But for all his successes, Shapey was still struggling to make ends meet. Having returned to his job at the Third Street Settlement, he decided to approach the director for a raise. The result was disastrous. Recalls Shapey: "I walked into his office and demanded a raise. He refused. So I leaned down onto his desk and said, 'Then you can take this job and shove it up your ass,' and walked out. Now I had a wife, a son, and no job."

During the next several months Shapey made a meager living teaching a few private students. He had begun charging a fee for his services as a conductor, but of course, the fees were paltry. Vera worked for a while as a switchboard operator, until her pregnancy became too far advanced. "She continued to make some money from her paintings, but in looking back on it all and trying to figure it out," says Ralph, "I still don't know how Vera and I managed on what we made."

Then, in the spring of 1962, he received a call from George Rochberg at the University of Pennsylvania. Rochberg explained to Ralph that he had just been appointed chairman of the music department, and wanted to know if Ralph would take a part-time position as conductor of both the chorus and orchestra. A few days later he was offered a grant to lecture at Princeton University for one semester. The prestige of Princeton beckoned to Shapey and he wanted to do both, but schedule conflicts between the two made that impossible. Of course, Ralph chose the position at the University of Pennsylvania, and for one year he commuted to Philadelphia from New York, in a small used car, for an annual salary of about four thousand dollars.

But in 1963, Shapey was visited in New York by the pianist Easley Blackwood. Says Shapey: "Blackwood had brought a tape recording with him, and asked if he could play it for me, wanting to know what I thought of it. It was a recently-written work by a famous composer, and—I didn't know this until later—with Blackwood at the piano. So I listened to it. After it was over I told Blackwood that the playing of it was a real tour de force. But the piece was a piece of shit. It didn't go anywhere and it didn't say anything; it was little more than an exercise. Little did I know, Blackwood was on the search committee from the University of Chicago. They were looking for a composer to start and direct a contemporary chamber group. I guess I impressed him. A short time later the committee asked me to come to Chicago for an interview.

"I went to my dear friend Henry Weinberg and told him I had my doubts about moving to Chicago. I didn't see a purpose in going to all the trouble of sending scores and a resume; I didn't think I stood a chance of getting the job. But Weinberg told me to go. He said the opportunity was too good to pass up, that *of course* I was going to go through with sending all those materials. So I sent them, and I went to the interview."

After a preliminary interview with the faculty, Shapey went before Dean Streeter and Leonard B. Meyer, an old friend of Shapey's who was now the chairman of the music department. (At the time, Shapey suspected that Meyer had pulled strings to get him the interview. But in later years he learned that the search committee's nominations were department-wide and unbiased.)

The interview with the faculty went well. But by the time Shapey made it to the Dean's office he was weary of the protocol involved in this selection process. With Dean Streeter and Mr. Meyer, the question and answer period of a fairly typical interview was in progress with Dean Streeter going on about something, when Ralph suddenly interrupted him and said impatiently: "Look, gentlemen, let's get one thing straight. I have no intention of becoming a dusty book on one of your shelves. I'm a revolutionary. I'm against a lot of what goes on at universities, and if I get this job you'll have me fighting things from the inside."

Then Shapey stopped, looked at the two surprised men staring back at him, took a deep breath, and said: "Well, I guess I just talked myself out of a job," when suddenly Streeter doubled up his fist and banged it down hard on his desk exclaiming: "That's what we stand for! That's what we stand for at this university!" A short time later Shapey was appointed.

Shapey had returned to New York to wind up his commitments there and to prepare for his move to Chicago. He had been back in New York for about one month when he got a phone call from Leonard Meyer, congratulating him. The Contemporary Chamber Players and its new conductor (Shapey) had just been awarded a Rockefeller Foundation Grant for which he, Leonard, had applied some months earlier.

"Thanks a lot, Leonard," said Ralph, "but I don't deserve any congratulations; I didn't have a thing to do with it."

"That is so," replied Meyer, "but you're going to be walking around with a quarter of a million bucks in your pocket."

Before leaving New York, Norman Lloyd, then head of the Rockefeller Foundation, sent for Shapey. After some congratulations and small talk, Mr. Lloyd said: "Ralph, we're sending you to Chicago because, as far as contemporary music is concerned, the place is a desert. Your job is to make it bloom."

When Shapey first arrived, he conducted the Contemporary Chamber Players and taught a course in analysis and composition. Soon after, because of the successes of the Contemporary Chamber Players, he taught only private composition and a course in conducting for composers.

The Contemporary Chamber Players gave their first concert December 1, 1964, to a packed house. The program included works by Schoenberg, Webern, Berg, Davidowsky, and Varese. The players—by audition—were the best free-lance musicians in Chicago. Shapey recalls that the players "had sort of heard of the terrible Schoenberg,

Webern, and Berg. The younger ones had never heard of Varese."

From March 3 to April 2 of that year, the Contemporary Chamber Players toured New York City (Carnegie Hall) and Philadelphia, where they played an all-Varese concert in celebration of his eightieth birthday. Says Shapey: "Donald Henahan was critic then, and he gave us tremendous publicity, photos, write-ups, interviews, and rave reviews. The auditorium was packed; they were hanging from the rafters. Even Jean Martinon came to my concerts!"

At that time the provost of the University of Chicago was Edward Levy, the brilliant lawyer who later became President of the University and then U. S. Attorney General under the Ford Administration. After the concert Shapey was standing in a corner of the reception room chatting with Meyer when Mr. Levy approached him. He congratulated Shapey on the performance, then took him aside, saying: "Ralph, your job here is to make this department famous, and I'll give you anything you need or want to do it."

Two years later, Paul Fromm, a friend of Shapey's since 1960, invited Shapey to his apartment in Chicago. They had dinner together, after which Fromm informed Shapey that he had been observing the Contemporary Chamber Players for the past two years to see what Ralph would do with them. He told Ralph that he was very pleased, and that from then on, Ralph was to include a Fromm concert on his series. The Fromm foundation would provide the funding.

On February 21, 1967, the Fromm concert was to feature Gaburo's *Antiphony No. 3,* Carter's Double Concerto for Harpsichord, Piano, and Two Chamber Orchestras, and Shapey's *Dimensions*—his second work for the season on the Contemporary Chamber Players series. Shapey objected, citing his own rule that a staff member was not permitted to have more than one work per season, and that his Concerto for Clarinet and Chamber Group had been performed just last October. But Paul Fromm insisted that it was his concert, his money, and he wanted all the works that he had recently commissioned to be on the program. Consequently, Ralph's rule was rescinded, and *Dimensions* was performed.

The Fromm concerts continued even after Mr. Fromm's death in 1987, thanks to a legacy of $150,000, which lasted for nine years. The last Fromm concert, celebrating Ralph's seventy-fifth birthday, took place April 14, 1996. It was dedicated to Joan Greenstone, beloved daughter of Paul and Erika Fromm, who died on February 22, 1996. The program consisted of Schoenberg's *Chamber Symphony, Op. 9;* Session's *Concertino,* and Shapey's *Incantations.* "It's unfortunate," says Shapey, "Those concerts were always jam-packed."

By 1969 Shapey had written six string quartets, seven works for orchestra, twenty-five works for various chamber groups, and fifteen keyboard works. His compositions were featured on nine recordings released by CRI. Seven years after the inception of the Contemporary Chamber Players, Shapey went to New York to ask the Rockefeller Foundation for another $250,000. With virtually no red tape, they gave it to him.

Despite these successes, Shapey was troubled. Anyone who has known him will attest to his coarse, outspoken language and rugged manners. He once said, "I don't want anybody to think I'm religious. I'm irreligious." But if he is not religious, he is certainly spiritual, as implied in the titles of many of his instrumental compositions (*Convocations, Incantations, Rituals*), and he has employed texts from the Old Testament in many of his vocal works (*This Day for Female Voice and Piano, Songs of Ecstasy, Praise, The Songs of Eros, Song of Songs* trilogy, and *The Covenant,* to name a few). Moreover, he has always held to the uncompromising belief that music should not be judged in conjunction with the personality and image of the artist who creates it. Detailed program notes on modern music have upset Shapey, who feels that they are too often excuses for the music. He has frequently stated that a composer's music must stand on its own merit.

Added to these conflicts was the turmoil of the Vietnam War, which Shapey vehemently opposed. It was the combination of all these elements that led him, in 1969, to announce a moratorium on all his music, forbidding performances of it anywhere. Generally, he offered little or no comment on his decision. When asked, he would reply that it was "for personal and political reasons. I was growing increasingly disgusted with the world in general and the music world in particular." When I asked Ralph about it recently, he replied: "Basically, I went out on strike against the Vietnam War and all of the rotten (I felt) actions of our society. Many composers, friends, and foes called and told me: 'Only you have the guts to make such a statement!'" In her article "Why This Oratorio," Ann Noren writes:

> For a man with a strong local reputation for being outspoken, Shapey's cryptic silence on this subject may seem uncharacteristic. With due prodding, he may confide his reason, but it is not for publication. The off-the-record answer he gives, however, reflects an understanding of human nature that goes back at least as far as Socrates, if not Moses.[5]

In 1976, seven years after he announced the moratorium, Shapey's friend Paul Fromm came to see him. Often, Fromm had tried to talk Shapey into ending the silence. On this particular visit, "Paul said to me: 'These works are your children, and you have to let your children live. One cannot be involved with the entire human race. There are many who want to hear and be part of your music. Why do you deny them?' I had never thought of my music in those terms, but I decided that he was right."

The moratorium on his music ended on Saturday, February 28, 1976, in Rockefeller Chapel at the University of Chicago with the premiere of *Praise,* written during his moratorium. (He had never stopped composing.) The concert was covered by the Chicago papers, and Shapey's piece received the usual enthusiastic reviews.

According to Shapey, the biggest surprise in his life came in 1982. "I remember it was a Thursday afternoon, around four-thirty or five o'clock. I was composing, the phone rang, and a fellow introduced himself as Mr. Corbaly from the MacArthur Foundation. He asked if I knew anything about the foundation. I said 'No, I don't,' which was true. The reason I had never heard of them is because they had never done anything in music to my knowledge. So he told me about the foundation and that I had just been awarded a fellowship, and that I was about to be given some money. I said to him, 'Well, what's the catch? Do I have to leave my job?' Mr. Corbaly replied, 'No, you don't.' I asked him: 'Well, do I have to compose anything special?' 'No, no, you don't. You're simply being handed a large sum of money.' Then I got annoyed, and I said 'All right. Which one of my enemies or friends put you up to this gag?' It took awhile, but Mr. Corbaly finally convinced me that the offer was genuine, and that the next day I would get all the information in the mail, which did occur. What's more, it turned out that Mr. Corbaly was using a speaker phone, and everyone in the office heard the conversation. This is one of the most famous stories at the Foundation."

In 1985, Ralph married Elsa Charlston, who had been the soprano soloist with the Contempo-

---

[5]From an interview with Ann Noren, *Chicago Sun Times,* Feb. 22, 1976.

rary Chamber Players since 1970. Also in that year Shapey was offered a temporary position as Distinguished Professor at Queens College. He taught at the CUNY Graduate Center on 42nd St. as well, and conducted the Queens College Contemporary Players (which group Ralph created). But Ralph was now sixty-five years old. The long commute, and the many flights of stairs he found necessary to climb were too strenuous for his heart. He was offered a permanent position, but he declined and returned to Chicago the following year.

After returning to Chicago, Shapey received three of his most prestigious honors, the last of which produced a scandal in the music world. In 1987, Shapey was given a commission by the Philadelphia Orchestra, for which he composed the *Symphony Concertante.* ("Muti loved that piece," recalls Shapey.) Shapey saw Muti at La Scala the following year, and Muti hugged him. Ralph said, "We made a noise in Philadelphia," and Muti replied, "A *good* noise!" In 1990, Shapey was awarded the Kennedy Friedheim award for his Concerto for Cello, Piano, and String Orchestra. And in 1991, he composed the *Concerto Fantastique* for the Chicago Symphony, commissioned for the dual centennial of the Chicago Symphony Orchestra and the University of Chicago.

The *Concerto Fantastique* was submitted to judges of the Pulitzer Committee—which included George Perle, Harvey Sollberger, and Roger Reynolds—who awarded Shapey the Pulitzer Prize in music. But about two hours after being notified of the award, he was contacted by the Pulitzer Committee and informed that it was being taken away.[6] In recalling the incident, Ralph said with exasperation, "Now why bother having judges if you're not going to listen to them? These guys submitted their recommendation to the committee, and the committee decided to override it." In the presence of the press, one newspaper critic asked the chairman of the board why the prize was rescinded. He replied, "We had to take into consideration consumer interest." That critic called Ralph for a comment. His answer was: "If it's for consumer interest, then they should put the Pulitzer Prize for Music in K-Mart."

For days Shapey's phone rang incessantly, and he received stacks of mail. His publisher Arnold Broido called him and said, "Don't feel too bad, Ralph, you got a million dollars worth of publicity out of it."

"Even my enemies—and I've got plenty of them—were up in arms over the incident," Ralph said. "But what can you do? As far as I'm concerned, the Board can take their goddamn prize and shove it."

Shapey, of course, continued to compose, conduct, and to receive commissions and reverent reviews for his premieres. It was business as usual. His accomplishments up to this point had been extraordinary for a contemporary composer. And yet, over the next six years he would receive his three most prestigious honors. In 1989 he was elected to the American Academy of Arts and Letters; in 1993 he was given the Paul Fromm award for his contribution to modern music; and in 1994 he was elected to the American Academy of Arts and Sciences.

Ralph turned seventy in 1991. There were numerous articles written and concerts given across the country. At that time, in accordance with Federal laws on the age limits of college professors, Ralph was asked to retire. He had been at the University of Chicago twenty-seven years.

---

[6]The rescinding of a Pulitzer had occurred once before in literature (*Gravity's Rainbow,* by Anthony Pynchon).

He had more than achieved the task set before him by Edward Levy: the contemporary music scene at Chicago under Ralph's direction had become known throughout most of the world, and the music department had twice been rated as the best in the country.

Shapey continues to compose. Even at this writing he is rendering the accompanying catalogue incomplete. The Naumberg Foundation commissioned his Eighth String Quartet, and the University of Wisconsin commissioned his Ninth for the Pro Arte String Quartet. The listing of compositions since 1993 was added after the manuscript for this book was submitted to Pendragon for publication; in fact, Shapey phoned me just recently, telling me that he has been cleaning house and has come across a large number of works he thought were lost. It makes me think that the hardest part about working with—or writing about—Shapey is keeping up with him. Currently, his entire collection of manuscripts is in the process of being turned over to the University of Chicago's Regenstein Library, Special Collections.

I had the privilege of taking a rather looseknit seminar from Ralph at the Graduate Center in New York during his stint at Queens College. (Professors at the one often teach doctoral courses at the other.) Ralph treated his students with gentleness, cited his favorite maxims frequently and with relish, and often laughed hardest at his own jokes. Dan Dorff, an editor at Presser, once studied with Shapey at Tanglewood in the 1970's. He recalls: "In a class where the students were tapping and singing their rhythm and melody exercises for Shapey, one student once made a mistake and muttered 'Shoot!' 'Shoot?' exclaimed Ralph, in a loud voice. *'Shoot?'* And with a look of both exasperation and warmth, he said: 'You meant *shit,* didn't you? Let me tell you something, son: If you can't say what you mean, do us all a favor and don't compose music.'"

General descriptions of his compositional style (the concepts of "it is" and the "Graven Image") have been discussed often enough in other writings and will not be repeated here.[7] And his favorite quote—that "great art is a miracle"—has been used often enough as a conclusion to writings on Shapey. So I told Ralph I would like to conclude his biography with the description of his music he favors most, and with anything else he would care to add. He replied: "Well, the 12-tone composers have wanted nothing to do with me. Nor did the neoclassicists, and certainly not the minimalists. Bach, Mozart, Beethoven, and Brahms are my gods...I'd give my right arm to be able to write music like that. I use traditional forms: concerto, sonata, and so on. Also I am a romantic, but romanticism is a dirty word. It seems every composer has to fit into a cubbyhole, and it was Leonard Meyer and later the critic Bernard Jacobson who called me what I really am: a radical traditionalist. When younger composers in New York and Chicago gave concerts titled, 'The New Romantics,' I was called by the press and asked why I wasn't included. I answered: 'I guess because I'm an old Romantic.'

"Another thing people often ask me is, 'Why do you write such difficult music? Is it to challenge the performer or the audience?' and I reply: 'Neither one. I write to challenge myself; if I don't, I die!'

"At their first composition lesson with me, I tell my students: 'from this day forward you have only the right to *know.* Don't ever come and tell

---

[7] c.f. Cole Gaganey and Tracey Caras' *Soundpieces: Interviews With Amercian Composers* and John Rockwell's *All American Music: Composition in the Late Twentieth Century,* both cited in the bibliography.

me of like or dislike. They are meaningless. Today we dislike, tomorrow we like, and vice versa.'

"I have a list of books which I give to my students to read—not just for the years they study with me, but for their lifetime. And very few of those books are about music. I insist that the tools of technique are absolutely necessary for good composition. One must be a 'Master' at whatever one does—composer, conductor, instrumentalist, or what have you—in order to be able to say what one wants to say. But it is what is inside of me as a human being that will make my music worthwhile. If I am empty inside, then my music will be empty, and I am just a technician writing exercises.

"I don't consider writing to be a God-given gift. I guess I'm a Deist, like Jefferson. I believe there is a God (creative force), and that this force created the universe. But I also believe that it has since gone about its business, and has little to do with us. Waiting for this force to give us something to say in our music is nonsense. I must become rich from within. And the only way to make myself rich is by study and learning. The most upsetting thing about my life is how little I know. I'm not being humble; this really upsets me, because there is so much to learn, and so little time left to do so.

"As for my recent style, I'm still writing from my worksheet, my cantus firmus, which I call my 'Mother Lode.'[8] Not long ago, Joel Krosnick said to me: 'Ralph, this isn't a Mother Lode, it's an *Elsa Lode*. And I don't understand how you do it! All these pieces built from the same material, yet each one sounds different!'

"I created my Mother Lode worksheet, which contains my cantus firmus with harmonic aggregates assigned to each cantus note. It is constructed so that there are always common tones from any one aggregate to another. As in traditional tonal practice, this allows me to easily shift from one aggregate to another, no matter how distant these aggregates are from each other. The aggregates are lettered 'A' to 'F,' with 'F' being the cantus, while 'A' is the cantus in retrograde. Because of this flexibility, I have written to date sixty-five works based on this worksheet. It so far seems to lend itself to any and all musical manipulations towards writing work after work.

"And lately I've been doing some very interesting things with it. One thing I'll do is start with two and go to eleven,[9] then use twelve and one—or vice versa—to build the coda. Sometimes I break it into groups of two, four, or six. So far, it has not failed me.

"Last summer at Tanglewood my *Evocation No. 2* for Cello, Piano, and Percussion was performed, and one of the Boston critics saved me for the last paragraph in his review and put me in stone. He said, 'If ever there is a Mount Rushmore for American composers, Shapey will be up there with Ruggles and Ives.'"

Sunday, April 14, 1996, Ralph conducted the final Fromm concert at Mandel Hall at the University of Chicago.[10] As for composing, Ralph says: "As long as I've got a brain left, and a hand and arm that works, I'll never stop."

---

[8] c.f. Appendix "Shapey's Compositional Method: The Mother Lode."

[9] Ibid.

[10] The program consisted of Schoenberg's Chamber Symphony No. 1 in E, Op. 9 (1906), Session's *Concertino* (1971), and Shapey's *Incantations* (1961). The latter two were commissioned by the Fromm Foundation.

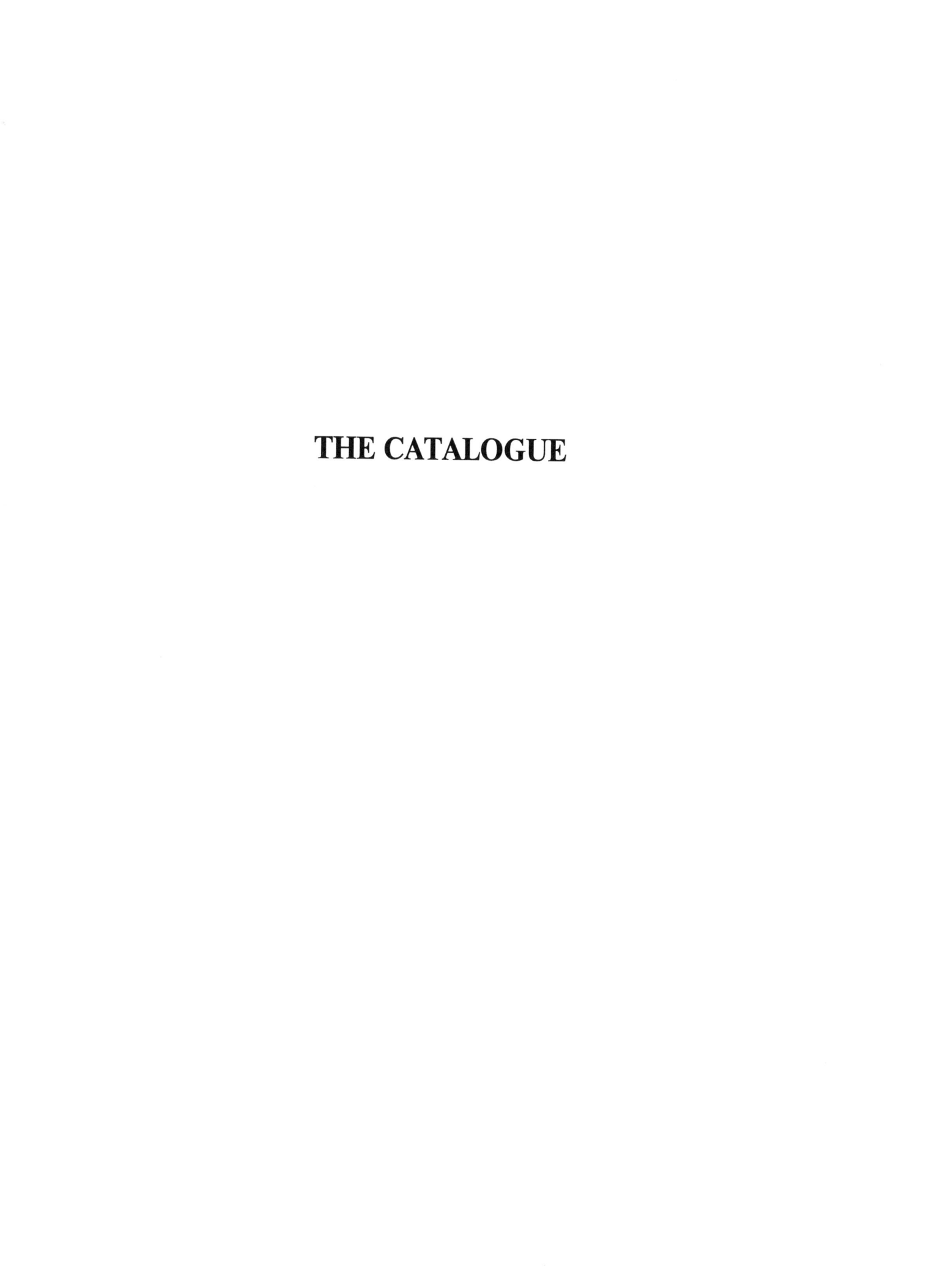

THE CATALOGUE

THE CATALOGUE

1 *Inspiration*

Medium:
Orchestra (r.s.)

Movements:
Single movement (no duration given) (r.s.)

Date:
1939.

Final copy:
Cannot locate (r.s.)

Dedication:
None (r.s.)

First Performance:
Tuesday, November 28, 1939, National Youth Administration Center, Philadelphia. National Youth Administration Orchestra, Ralph Shapey, Cond.

Reviews and Articles:
Philadelphia Evening Public Ledger, Tue., Nov. 28, 1939.

Publication:
Not published (r.s.)

Notes:
The only reference to this composition was found in the above article which consists of a brief mention of the upcoming performance with no details given.

2 *String Quartet No. 1*

Medium:
2 Vln., Vla., Vlc.

Movements:
I-Allegro moderato; II-Andante; III-Scherzo; IV-Maestoso

Date:
1946.

Final copy:
77 pp., ink on tissue.

First Performance:
Monday, October 31, 1983, Merkin Concert Hall, New York City. The Alard String Quartet: Joanne Zagst and Donald Hopkins, vln.; Raymond Page, vla.; Leonard Feldman, vcl.

Reviews and Articles:
The New York Times, Thu., Nov. 3, 1983.

Publication:
Rental - (no serial no.) (no duration given).

Notes:
The gap between compositions (1939–46) is due to Shapey's years in military service.

3 *Sonata No. 1 for Piano*

Medium:
Pn.

Movements:
I-Allegro moderato; II-Scherzo: allegro, trio; III-Adagio appassionata (no duration given).

Date:
1946.

Final Copy:
24 pp., ink on tissue.

Dedication:
Dedicated to Shirley Aronoff.

First Performance:
None (r.s.)

Reviews and Articles:
None (r.s.)

Publication:
Withdrawn.

4   *Quintet for String Quartet and Piano*

Medium:
   2 Vln., Vla., Vcl., Pn.

Movements:
   I-Allegro; II-Passacaglia (45′).

Date:
   3/47.

Final Copy:
   84 pp., ink on tissue.

Dedication:
   To "Joy."

First Performance:
   Not known.

Publication:
   Published - special order - 114405650.

---

5   *Three Essays on Thomas Wolf for Piano*

Medium:
   Pn.

Movements:
   I-Adagio maestoso; II-Largo; III-Allegro (no duration given).

Date:
   9/1/48.

Final Copy:
   47 pp., ink on tissue.

First Performance:
   Friday, October 5, 1984, Eastman School of Music, Rochester, NY. Lisa Moore, pn., Private concert (not open to the public) (r.s.)

Reviews and Articles:
   None (r.s.)

Publication:
   Published - 41041236. None.

Notes:
   The dates given in the Presser brochure of Shapey's works give the dates 1948–49. The above date, however, is the only date appearing on the ink-on-tissue final copy.

6   *String Quartet No. 2*

Medium:
   2 Vln., Vla., Vcl.

Movements:
   Single movement in four sections, labeled Allegro moderato, Adagio, Passacaglia, Scherzo (12′ 30″).

Date:
   1/18/49.

Final Copy:
   25 pp., ink on tissue. (6′)

First Performance:
   Monday, March 27, 1950, Times Hall, New York City. Juilliard String Quartet: Robert Mann and Robert Koff, vln.; Raphael Hillyer, vla.; Artur Winnograd, vcl.

Reviews and Articles:
   (P) *The New York Times,* Tue., Mar. 28, 1950. (P) *New York Herald Tribune,* Tue., Mar. 28, 1950.

Publication:
   Published - special order - 114405710.

Notes:
   There is a second copy on vellum in sepia ink. The sepia ink is on the reverse side of the printed staffs. On the same side as the printed staffs the time signatures are drawn in pencil.

---

7   *Sonata for Violin and Piano*

Medium:
   Vln., Pn.

Movements:
   I-Largo maestoso; II-Scherzo; III-Rubato (no duration given).

Date:
   1/8/50.

Final Copy:
   28 pp., ink on tissue.

Publication:
   Published - special order - 001301.

First Performance:

None (r.s.)

Reviews and Articles:

None (r.s.)

---

8 *String Quartet No. 3*

Medium:

2 Vln., Vla., Vcl.

Movements:

I-Allegro - adagio; II-Adagio; III-Quasi scherzo; IV-q=52 (no duration given).

Date:

1/31/50–1/20/51, New York City.

Final Copy:

113 pp., ink on tissue.

Publication:

Rental - (no serial no.)

First Performance:

None (r.s.)

Reviews and Articles:

None (r.s.)

---

9 *Seven Little Pieces for Piano*

Medium:

Pn.

Movements:

Seven one-page pieces (8').

Date:

1951.

Final Copy:

11 pp., engraved.

Publication:

Published - 41041222.

First Performance:

None (r.s.)

---

10 *Cantata*

Medium:

Sop., Ten., and Bass Soli, Narrator, 1.1.1.1 - 2.1.1.1, Pc., Str.

Movements:

Single movement (30').

Date:

1/22/51–6/17/51.

Final Copy:

94 pp., pencil on tissue.

Publication:

Rental - 0131039.

Dedication:

To my father.

First Performance:

None (r.s.)

Reviews and Articles:

None (r.s.)

Notes:

Source of text: Sylvia Shapey (= wife): written specifically for Shapey's Cantata (unpublished).

---

11 *Fantasy for Symphony Orchestra*

Medium:

3.3.3.3.- 3.3.3.1., Timp., Pc., Pn.

Movements:

Single movement (no duration given).

Date:

7/9/51–8/28/51.

Final Copy:

59 pp., ink on tissue.

Publication:

Withdrawn.

Dedication:

None (r.s.)

First Performance:

None (r.s.)

Notes:

Honorable mention, Gershwin Contest, NY, 1951. This competition no longer exists. Shapey cannot remember who sponsored it. However he does recall that Dimitri Mitropoulos presented the awards and conducted a performance of the winning work.

---

12 *Sonata for Oboe and Piano*

Medium:

Ob., Pn.

Movements:

I-q=44; II-8th=192; III-q=40; IV-q=100 (18′).

Date:

11/11/51-2/26/52.

Final Copy:

42 pp., ink on tissue.

Publication:

Published - special order - 114405700.

First Performance:

None (r.s.) Recordings:

CRI SD 501.

Notes:

Commissioned by Josef Marx.

---

13 *Suite of Four Pieces for Piano*

Medium:

Pn.

Movements:

Single movement in four sections, labeled I-IV (no duration given).

Date:

3/5/52-4/20/52.

Final Copy:

7 pp., ink on tissue.

Publication:

Published - special order - 110406940.

Dedication:

To Jack Maxin.

First Performance:

None (r.s.)

Reviews and Articles:

None (r.s.)

Notes:

Title on final copy reads: Suite for Piano.

---

14 *Symphony No. 1*

Medium:

3.3.3.3.- 4.3.3.1., 3 Pc., Pn., Str.

Movements:

Single movement (no duration given).

Date:

5/19/52-8/26/52, New York City.

Final Copy:

82 pp., ink on tissue.

Publication:

Published - special order - 001318.

First Performance:

None (r.s.)

Reviews and Articles:

None (r.s.)

---

15 *Oboe Quartet for Oboe, Violin, Viola, and Cello*

Medium:

Ob., Vln., Vla., Vcl.

Movements:

I-q=56-58; II-Leggiero (q[tied to]16th=60) (10′).

Date:

11/2/52-12/18/52.

Final Copy:

26 pp., ink on tissue.

Publication:

Published - special order - 114405640.

Dedication:

To Josef Marx.

First Performance:

Monday, October 31, 1983, Merkin Concert Hall, New York City. James Ostryniec, ob. and members of the Alard String Quartet: Joanne Zagst, vln.; Raymond Page, vla.; Leonard Feldman, vcl.

---

16   *String Quartet No. 4*

Medium:

2 Vln., Vla., Vcl.

Movements:

I-Maestoso; II-Leggiero, sempre spiccato e piano; III-Allegro, non legato, maestoso (12').

Date:

6/4/53-9/9/53.

Final Copy:

37 pp., ink on tissue (16').

Publication:

Published - special order - 114405720.

Dedication:

Commissioned by and dedicated to Alma Morgenthau.

First Performance:

Wednesday, May 26, 1954, Kaufman Auditorium, YM-YWHA, 92 St., New York City. Broadus Earle & Matthew Raimondi, vln.; Walter Trampler, vla.; Claus Adam, vcl.

Reviews and Articles:

(P) *The New York Times,* Thu., May 27, 1954.

---

17   *Sonata for Cello and Piano*

Medium:

Vcl., Pn.

Movements:

I-Andante cantabile; II-Moderato leggiero; III-Con moto (14').

Date:

I & II: 10/15/53-11/13/53, London; III: 12/19/53-1/1/54, Munich.

Final Copy:

32 pp., ink on tissue, most dynamics and several other markings in pencil.

Publication:

Published - special order - 11440569.

First Performance:

Saturday, March 10, 1956, Carnegie Recital Hall, New York City. Jackson Wiley, vcl.; Russell Sherman, pn.

Reviews and Articles:

(P) *The New York Times,* Sun., Mar. 11, 1956.

Notes:

Composed in Europe under the Frank Huntington Beebe Scholarship Award.

---

18   *Piece in the Form of   Sonata-Variations for Piano*

Medium:

Pn.

Movements:

Theme and variations in ten sections (12' 40").

Date:

1/2/54-2/15/54, Munich.

Final Copy:

29 pp., ink on tissue, dynamics and some phrase markings in pencil.

Publication:

Published - special order - 110406960.

First Performance:

(NY Premiere) Saturday, October 13, 1956, Carnegie Recital Hall, New York City. Lalan Parrott, Pn.

Reviews and Articles:

The New York Times, Sun., Oct. 14, 1956.

Notes:

Composed in Europe under the Frank Huntington Beebe Scholarship award.

19   *Concerto for Clarinet and Chamber Group*

Medium:
Cl. Solo; Hn., Pc., Pn., Vln., Vcl.

Movements:
Single movement (11' 30").

Date:
3/24/54–6/7/54.

Final Copy:
39 pp., ink on tissue.

Publication:
Rental - 0150482.

Dedication:
To my wife, Sylvia.

First Performance:
Sunday, March 20, 1955, Philharmonic Chamber Ensemble, Kaufman Auditorium, YM-YWHA, 92 St., New York City. Stanley Drucker, cl.; M. Weiner, vln.; E. Bailey & W., pc.; A. Sophos, vcl.; J. Singer, hn.; A. Bogin, pn.; Ralph, Shapey, cond.

Reviews and Articles:
(P) *The New York Times,* Mon., Mar. 21, 1955.

20   *Trio for Violin, Cello, and Piano*

Medium:
Vln., Vcl., Pn.

Movements:
I-Maestoso, Allegro, Andante, Andante; II- Allegro; III- Andante (14' 30").

Date:
I - 2/8/53–4/16/53, II - 8/5/54–4/3/55, III - 4/14/55–5/2/55.

Final Copy:
59 pp., ink on tissue, dynamics and several expression markings in pencil.

Publication:
Published - special order - 114405660.

Dedication:
To Robert Adler.

First Performance:
Friday, May 22, 1959, Carl Fischer Concert Hall, New York City. Matthew Raimondi, vln.; Lorin Bersohn, vcl.; Lalan Parrott, pn.

Reviews and Articles:
San Francisco Chronicle, Tue., May 28, 1963. *San Francisco Examiner,* Tue., May 28, 1963.

Notes:
The concert at which the first performance took place consisted only of the works of Shapey and Stefan Wolpe. Five of Shapey's works were premiered that night: Trio for Violin, Cello, and Piano (entry no. 20), Piano Trio (entry no. 21), Rhapsodie for Oboe and Piano (entry no. 26), String Quartet No. 5 (entry no. 27), and Form for Piano (entry no. 33).

21   *Piano Trio*

Medium:
Vln., Vcl., Pno.

Movements:
I-Maestoso; II - Allegro; III-Andante IV-Andante (12').

Date:
4/14/55–5/8/55.

Final copy:
59 pp., ink on tissue.

Publication:
Published - special order - 114405660.

Dedication:
To Robert Adler.

First Performance:
Friday, May 22, 1959, Carl Fischer Concert Hall, New York City. Matthew Raimondi, vln.; Loren Bernsohn, vcl.; Lalan Parrott, pn.

Reviews and Articles:
None (r.s.)

Notes:
The concert at which the first performance took place consisted only of the works of Shapey and Stefan Wolpe. Five of Shapey's works were premiered that night: Trio for Violin, Cello, and

Piano (entry no. 20), Piano Trio (entry no. 21), Rhapsodie for Oboe and Piano (entry no. 26), String Quartet No. 5 (entry no. 27), and Form for Piano (entry no. 33).

22 *Challenge the Family of Man*

Medium:

4.4.4.4 - Eng. Hn., .3.3.1.1, Pc., Pn., Str.

Movements:

Single movement. I-8th=66 (1′ 55″); II-8th=168 (4′ 37″); III-8th=84 (4′ 45″); IV-8th=50 (2′ 14″); V=8th=66 (13′ 31″).

Date:

6/1/55–10/17/55.

Final copy:

39 pp., ink on tissue.

Publication:

Published - special order - 0110480.

Dedication:

To Dimitri Mitropoulos.

First Performance:

Thursday, February 9, 1956, Carnegie Hall, New York City. Philharmonic Symphony Society of New York, Dimitri Mitropoulos, cond.

Notes:

Title page states "In one movement." However, the score is marked off with roman numerals and durations at ends of sections.

23 *Short Piece for Piano Solo*

Medium:

Pn.

Movements:

Single movement (1′ 10″).

Date:

9/9/56, MacDowell Colony, NH.

Final copy:

3 pp., ink on tissue.

Publication:

Published - special order - (no Presser cat. no.).

First Performance:

None (r.s.)

Notes:

Written on cover page in Shapey's hand: "Based on the following notes: C, E♭, F, F#, D, E. Given at dinner 9/7/56 by the following persons: Composers Copland, Allenbrook, La Montaine, Shapey, music critic Hughes, writer MacDonald (one note per person)." Shapey recalls that when those in attendance expressed their astonishment at this feat, he replied "What's the big deal? You gave me more notes to work with than I generally give myself!" (Conversation with Ralph Shapey, April, 1993).

24 *Mutations I for Piano*

Medium:

Pn.

Movements:

Eight pages in eight sections, labeled I-VIII (6′ 30″).

Date:

6/23/56–7/31/56, New York City.

Final copy:

8 pp., ink on tissue.

Dedication:

To Irma Wolpe-Radamacher.

Publication:

Published - special order - 110406880.

First Performance:

Sunday, April 6, 1958, The Nonagon, Second Ave., New York City. Composer's Showcase Concert Series, Irma Wolpe, pn.

Reviews and Articles:

(P) *New York Herald Tribune,* Mon., Apr. 7, 1958.
(P) *The New York Times,* Mon., Apr. 7, 1958.

25   *Duo for Viola and Piano*

Medium:

Vla., Pn.

Movements:

Single movement in five sections labeled Andante con espressivo - quasi cadenza - leggiero - andante con espressivo - maestoso (9′ 20″).

Date:

1957.

Final copy:

17 pp., ink on tissue, most dynamic and expression marks in pencil.

Publication:

Published - special order - 114405590.

Dedication:

To Winterry.

First Performance:

Wednesday, March 26, 1958, Third Street Music School Settlement, New York City. Walter Trampler, vla.; Lalan Parrott, pn. (r.s.)

26   *Rhapsodie for Oboe and Piano*

Medium:

Ob., Pn.

Movements:

Single movement (5′ 30″).

Date:

6/14/57, New York City-7/21/57, MacDowell Colony, NH.

Final copy:

12 pp., ink on tissue.

Publication:

Published - special order - 114405680.

First Performance:

Friday, May 22, 1959, Carl Fischer Concert Hall, New York City. Josef Marx, ob.; Lalan Parrott, pn.

Reviews and Articles:

The Washington Post, Tue., Nov. 8, 1983.

Recordings:

CRI SD 423.

Notes:

The concert at which the first performance took place consisted only of the works of Shapey and Stefan Wolpe. Five of Shapey's works were premiered that night: Trio for Violin, Cello, and Piano (entry no. 20), Piano Trio (entry no. 21), Rhapsodie for Oboe and Piano (entry no. 26), String Quartet No. 5 (entry no. 27), and Form for Piano (entry no. 33).

27   *String Quartet No. 5 with Female Voice*

Medium:

Sop., 2 Vln., Vla., Vcl.

Movements:

Single movement. However, penciled in and then erased are Roman numerals for 2nd and 3rd mvts. on pp. 8 & 16 (12′).

Date:

9/1/57, MacDowell Colony, NH-3/20/58, New York City.

Final copy:

27 pp., ink on tissue, voice and piano transcription included, also ink on tissue.

Publication:

Published - special order - 111401200. None.

Dedication:

To Vera (= Mrs. Shapey).

First Performance:

Friday, May 22, 1959, Carl Fischer Concert Hall, New York City. Valerie Lamoree, sop.; Matthew Raimondi and Nancy Cirillo, vln.; Theodore Israel, vla.; Lorin Bernsohn, vcl.

Reviews and Articles:

The Philadelphia Enquirer, Sun., May 27, 1962.

Notes:

The concert at which the first performance took place consisted only of the works of Shapey and Stefan Wolpe. Five of Shapey's works were premiered that night: Trio for Violin, Cello, and Piano (entry no. 20), Piano Trio (entry no. 21),

Rhapsodie for Oboe and Piano (entry no. 26), String Quartet No. 5 (entry no. 27), and Form for Piano (entry no. 33). Source of text: Vera Klement (=wife); written specifically for Shapey's String Quartet No. 5 (unpublished).

28 Sonata Variations for Piano

Medium:
Pn.

Movements:
Single movement (no duration given) (r.s.)

Date:
3/13/57.

Final copy:
Could not locate (r.s.)

Publication:
Not published.

Dedication:
None (r.s.)

First Performance:
Sunday, April 6, 1958, Third Street Music School Settlement, New York City.

Reviews and Articles:
(P) *New York Herald Tribune,* Mon., Apr. 7, 1958.
(P) *The New York Times,* Mon., Apr. 7, 1958.

29 Walking Upright

Medium:
Sop., Vln.

Movements:
Eight one-page songs (8′).

Date:
8/24/58–8/25/58, MacDowell Colony, NH.

Final copy:
8 pp., ink on tissue.

Publication:
Published - special order - 111401220.

First Performance:
Saturday, December 6, 1958, Third Street Music School Settlement, New York City. Faculty Concert Series, Paula Zwane, sop.; Matthew Raimondi, vln.

Notes:
Source of text: Vera Klement (=wife); written specifically for Shapey's *Walking Upright* (unpublished). Portions of this text are also used in Shapey's *The Covenant* (entry no. 70).

30 Ontogeny for Symphony Orchestra

Medium:
4.2.3.2 - 3.2.1.1, Pn., 9 Pc., Str.

Movements:
Single movement (20′).

Date:
6/18/58, New York City–8/20/58, Mac Dowell Colony, NH.

Final copy:
72 pp., ink on tissue.

Publication:
Rental - 0111218.

First Performance:
Saturday, May 1, 1965, Kleinhans Music Hall, State University of NY at Buffalo. The Buffalo Philharmonic Orchestra, Ralph Shapey, cond.

Reviews and Articles:
Chicago Tribune, Fri., May 27, 1966. *Chicago Daily News,* Fri., May 27, 1966. Henahan, Donal, "Current Chronical," *Musical Quarterly,* vol. 53, no. 2 (1967).

Notes:
On title page of ink-on-tissue copy: "Trilogy for Orchestra (Part I)."

31 Invocation - Concerto for Violin and Orchestra

Medium:
2.2.2.2.2 - 3.2.2.1, 3 Pc., Pn., Gui., Str.

Movements:
I-Maestoso; II-Recitative; III-With Joy (22′ 40″).

Date:

8/26/58, MacDowell Colony, NH–12/4/58, New York City.

Final copy:

86 pp., ink on tissue.

Publication:

Rental.

First Performance:

Friday, May 24, 1968, Mandel Hall, University of Chicago. Esther Glazer, vln.; Chicago Symphony Orchestra; Ralph Shapey, cond.

Reviews and Articles:

(P) *Chicago Daily News,* Mon., May 27, 1968. Henahan, Donal, "Current Chronical," *Musical Quarterly,* vol. 53, no. 2 (1967).

---

32   *Evocation No. 1 for Violin with Piano and Percussion*

Medium:

Vl., Pno., 1 Pc (3 Toms, Tam., B Dr., 2 Cym., Wd. Bl., Amelon, Sn., Sticks).

Movements:

I-Recitative—with intense majesty; II-With humor; III-With tenderness—with intense majesty—cadenza (18′).

Date:

1/59–4/59.

Final copy:

41 pp., engraved.

Publication:

Published - 414411610.

First Performance:

Saturday, March 26, 1960, Third Street Music School Settlement, New York City. Matthew Raimondi, vln.; Paul Price, pc.; Yehudi Wyner, pn.

Reviews and Articles:

The San Francisco Examiner, Tue., May 28, 1963. *The Boston Globe,* Wed., Jan. 28, 1981.

Disc review:

The New York Times, Sun., Apr. 27, 1975.

Recordings:

CRI SD 141.

---

33   *Form*

Medium:

Pn.

Movements:

Single movement (7′ 10″).

Date:

4/26/59–5/10/59.

Final copy:

8 pp., ink on tissue.

Publication:

Published - special order - 110406920.

First Performance:

Friday, May 22, 1959, Carl Fischer Concert Hall, New York City. David Tudor, pn.

Reviews and Articles:

Vassar Miscellany News, Poughkeepsie, NY, Wed., Nov. 8, 1961.

Notes:

The concert at which the first performance took place consisted only of the works of Shapey and Stefan Wolpe. Five of Shapey's works were premiered that night: Trio for Violin, Cello, and Piano (entry no. 20), Piano Trio (entry no. 21), Rhapsodie for Oboe and Piano (entry no. 26), String Quartet No. 5 (entry no. 27), and Form for Piano (entry no. 33).

---

34   *Soliloquy for Narrator, string quartet, and percussion*

Medium:

Narr., 2 Vln., Vla., Vcl., Pc.

Movements:

Single movement (11′ 18″).

Date:

7/6/59–7/18/59, MacDowell Colony, NH.

Final copy:

50 pp., ink on tissue.

Publication:

Rental - 0140482.

First Performance:

Friday, November 18, 1960, Kaufman Auditorium, YM-YWHA, 92 St., New York City. Music in Our Time concert series, Max Pollikoff, dir.; Hurd Hatfield, narr.; Gerald Tarack, vln.; Alan Martin, vln.; George (=Jorge) Mester, vla.; Aaron Shapinsky, vcl.; Paul Price, pc.; Ralph Shapey, cond.

Notes:

Source of text: Shakespeare: *Hamlet* ("To be or not to be.")

---

35 *Rituals for Symphony Orchestra*

Medium:

3.3.3.3, A. Sax., T. Sax., Bar. Sax.- 3.2.2.1, 8 Pc., Pn., Str.

Movements:

I-q=54; II-q=54, q=76, q=54 (12′ 55″).

Date:

7/25/59-8/15/59.

Final copy:

67 pp., ink on tissue.

Publication:

Score Published - 41641098.

First Performance:

Thursday, May 12, 1966. Mandel Hall, University of Chicago. Chicago Symphony Orchestra, Ralph Shapey, cond.

Reviews and Articles:

(P) *Chicago Daily News,* Fri., May 13, 1966, and Sat.-Sun., May 14-15, 1966. (P) *Chicago's American,* Fri., May 13, 1966. *The New York Times,* Sun., Oct. 31, 1971, and May 22, 1981. *Gramophone,* Sept. 1976.

Recordings:

CRI SD 275.

Notes:

(On title page) "This is the third work of a trilogy (Testament to Man) for orchestra: (I) ONTOGENY for Orch.; (II) INVOCATION— Concerto for Vln. and Orch.; (III) RITUALS. It was composed during the summer of 1959 at the MacDowell Colony in Petersborough, NH." Improvisational material for sax. given on p. 68.

---

36 *Movements for Woodwind Quintet*

Medium:

Fl., Ob., Cl., Hn., Bsn.

Movements:

I-Adagio; II-Moderato; III-Allegro (no duration given).

Date:

12/23/59-1/14/60.

Final copy:

23 pp., ink on tissue.

Publication:

Published - special order, parts: 11440563P, score: 11440563S.

First Performance:

Saturday, February 17, 1962, Dramatic Arts Center, Ann Arbor, MI. Dorian Woodwind Quintet: John Perras, fl.; David Pekett, ob.; Arthur Bloom, cl.; William Brown, hn.; Jane Taylor, bsn.

Reviews and Articles:

(P) *The Michigan Daily,* Sun., Feb. 18, 1962. (P) *The Ann Arbor News,* Mon., Feb. 19, 1962. *The New York Times,* Mon., Aug. 3, 1981.

---

37 *This Day for Female Voice and Piano*

Medium:

Sop., Pn.

Movements:

I-The Universe Resounds; II-Bone of My Bones; III-O Wonderful, Wonderful (4′).

Date:

2/3/60–2/9/60.

Final copy:

8 pp., ink on tissue.

Publication:

Published - special order - 111401210.

Dedication:

To My Wife Vera on the Birth of Our Son.

First Performance:

Saturday, April 24, 1965, Butler Auditorium, Capen Hall, State University of New York at Buffalo. Harriett Simons, mezzo sop.; Robert Marvel, pn.

Notes:

Sources of text: Vera Klement (=wife); written specifically for Shapey's "This Day" (unpublished). Old Testament: Isaiah. Shakespeare: *As You Like It*.

---

38 *De Profundis for Solo Doublebass and Instruments*

Medium:

Vln., Picc. (Fl.), Ob. (Eng. Hn.), Cl. (B. Cl., A.Sax), Hn.

Movements:

I-Recitative; II-Scherzo; III-Adagio–Moderato Grandioso (16′ 30″).

Date:

2/22/60–6/14/60.

Final copy:

28 pp., ink on tissue.

Publication:

Rental - 0150486.

Dedication:

To Bert Turetzky.

First Performance:

Wednesday, March 1, 1961, Hartt College of Music of the Univ. of Hartford. Hartt Chamber Players (performers not listed).

39 *Five for Violin and Piano*

Medium:

Vln., Pn.

Movements:

I-Recitative; II-Capriccio; III-Canto; IV-Scherzo (10′).

Date:

6/15/60–7/3/60.

Final copy:

21 pp., ink on tissue.

Publication:

Published - special order.

First Performance:

None (r.s.)

---

40 *Dimensions for Soprano and 23 Instruments*

Medium:

Sop., Fl., Picc., Ob., Eng. Hn., T. Sax., Hn., Tpt., Pn., 7 Pc., Timp., Db., (20′).

Movements:

I-q=44; II-q=48; III-q=40 (no duration given).

Date:

7/7/60–10/3/60, New York.

Final copy:

87 pp., ink on tissue.

Publication:

Rental - 0130482.

First Performance:

Saturday, May 13, 1962, New School, New York City. Bethany Beardsley, sop.

Reviews and Articles:

New York Herald Tribune, Sunday, May 14, 1962. *The Village Voice,* May 24, 1962. *San Francisco Sunday Chronicle,* Jun. 17, 1962.

Notes:

Source of Text: wordless syllables.

41 *Incantations for Soprano and Ten Instruments*

Medium:

Sop., A.Sax., Hn., Tpt., 2 Pc., Pn., Vcl.

Movements:

I-q=44; II-q=66; III-q=84; IV-8th=44 Recitative (in a thoughtful dream-like manner) (17′27″).

Date:

1961.

Final copy:

92 pp., ink on tissue.

Publication:

Rental - 411410960.

Dedication:

To Bethany Beardsley.

First Performance:

Saturday, April 22, 1961, Composer's Forum, Miller Hall, Columbia University, New York City. Bethany Beardsley, sop.

Reviews and Articles:

Chicago Daily News, Wed., Feb. 19, 1968. *The Seattle Times,* Fri., Mar 22, 1968. *Seattle Post-Intelligencer,* Sat., May 23, 1968. Disc reviews: *Christian Science Monitor,* Mon., May 12, 1969. *Stereo Review,* Aug, 1969. *High Fidelity Magazine,* Jun. 1969. *Stereo Review,* Aug. 1969. *American Record Guide,* Jul., 1969. *Chicago Sun Times,* Tue., Apr. 16, 1996. *Chicago Tribune,* Tuesday, April 16, 1996.

Recordings:

CRI SD 232.

Notes:

Text source: wordless vocalizations.

42 *Discourse I for Four Instruments*

Medium:

Fl., Cl., Pn., Vln.

Movements:

I-With great gesture; II-With intense wildness; III-With tenderness (13′ 5″).

Date:

7/12/61-8/11/61.

Final copy:

32 pp., ink on tissue, copyist.

Publication:

Published - special order - 0160488.

First Performance:

Wednesday, January 24, 1962, Town Hall, New York City. Aeolian Chamber Players, Harold Jones, fl.; Lewis Kaplan, vln.; Robert Listokin, cl.; Gilbert Kalish, pn.

Reviews and Articles:

(P) *The New York Times*, Thu., Jan. 25, 1962. *The New York Times,* Mon., Feb. 6, 1989.

43 *Convocation for Chamber Group*

Medium:

2 Ob., 2 Tpt., 2 Tmb., Bs. Tmb., 2 Vln., Db.

Movements:

Single movement (no duration given).

Date:

1/26/62-2/16/62, New York.

Final copy:

29 pp., ink on tissue.

Publication:

Rental - 0150484.

First Performance:

Unknown.

Reviews and Articles:

None (r.s.)

Notes:

"Was first performed in New York City, 5th Ave. Church, but [is] actually [the] opening of [the] large oratorio 'Praise' written many years later." (r.s.)

44 *Piece for Violin and Instruments*

Medium:

Ob., Cl., Bsn., Hn., Tpt., Tmb., Pc., Vcl.

Movements:

I-q=44; II-8th=44; III-q=80 (12′ 30″).

Date:

12/16/61–3/20/62.

Final copy:

14 pp., ink on tissue.

Publication:

Rental - 0150490

Dedication:

To Max Pollikoff.

First Performance:

Wednesday, May 9, 1962, Kaufman Auditorium, YM-YWHA, 92 St., New York City. Max Pollikoff, vln.

Notes:

The only available source of information regarding the premiere is a photocopy of a newspaper clipping found in Presser's collection of reviews and articles. The photocopy is of poor quality; the name of the newspaper and its exact date are not readable.

45 *Chamber Symphony for 10 Solo Players*

Medium:

Fl., Ob., E. Hn., Tpt., Hn., Pc., Pn., Vln., Vcl., Db.

Movements:

I-q=56; II-q=72; III-q=50 (11′).

Date:

7/15/62–9/29/62.

Final copy:

44 pp., ink on tissue.

Publication:

Published - special order - 0150480.

Dedication:

To my son, Max.

First Performance:

Monday, October 22, 1962, McMillin Academic Theatre, Columbia University, New York City. The Group for Contemporary Music: Harvey Sollberger, fl.; Josef Marx, ob.; Judith Martin, e.hn.; Albert Richman, hn.; Ronald Anderson, tpt.; Raymond Des Roches, pc.; Joan Tower, pc.; Jan Williams, pc.; Kenneth Goldsmith, vl.; William Rhein, db.; Charles Wourinen, pn.; Joel Krosnick, vcl.; Ralph Shapey, cond.

46 *Birthday Piece*

Medium:

Pn.

Movements:

Single movement (5′ 30″).

Date:

11/7/62–12/5/62.

Final copy:

7 pp., ink on tissue.

Publication:

Published - special order - 110406990.

Dedication:

See Notes.

First Performance:

Sunday, May 2, 1965, Twenty-Second American Music Festival, National Gallery of Art, Washington, D.C. Howard Lebow, pn.

Reviews and Articles:

(P) *The Evening Star* (Washington, D.C.), Mon., May 3, 1965. (P) *The Washington Post*, Mon., May 3, 1965.

Notes:

Title on ink-on-tissue copy reads "Birthday Piece for Stefan Wolpe for Piano."

47 *Seven for Piano Four Hands*

Medium:

Pn.

Movements:

Single movement (7′).

Date:

6/10/63–7/7/63.

Final copy:

18 pp., ink on tissue.

Publication:

Published - special order - 0160542.

Dedication:

To Milton and Peggy Salkind.

First Performance:

Monday, November 8, 1963, Hall of Flowers, Golden Gate Park, San Francisco. Milton and Peggy Salkind, pn.

Recordings:

Friends of Four Hand Piano Music.

Notes:

Commissioned by the artists.

---

48   *Brass Quintet*

Medium:

2 Tpt., Hn., 2 Tmb.

Movements:

I-q=52 (8th=104); II-16th=160; III-q=52 (8th=104) (12' 30").

Date:

6/30/62-7/9/63-7/22/63, Woodstock, NY.

Final copy:

28 pp., ink on tissue.

Publication:

Published - special order - 114406010.

Dedication:

To the American Brass Quintet.

First Performance:

Wednesday, Jan 27, 1975, Kaufman Auditorium, YM-YWHA, 92 St., New York City. The American Brass Quintet.

Reviews and Articles:

(P) *New Yorker,* Feb. 9, 1975.

Recordings:

New World Records, NW 377-2 (CD)

---

49   *String Quartet No. 6*

Medium:

2 Vln., Vla., Vcl.

Movements:

Single movement in six sections (11' 43").

Date:

7/26/63-8/21/63, Woodstock, NY.

Final copy:

13 pp., ink on tissue.

Publication:

Published - special order - 114405730.

Dedication:

To Harold and May Rosenberg (addition to dedication on final copy: "Written thanks to the Copley award and Stern Family Fund award. Dedicated to Harold Rosenberg and May Taball.")

First Performance:

Monday, November 28, 1966, Eisner and Lubin Auditorium, New York University, New York City. Matthew Raimondi & Anahid Ajemian, vln.; Bernard Zaslav, vla.; Seymor Barab, vcl.

Reviews and Articles:

(P) *The New York Times,* Tue., Nov. 29, 1966. Disc review: Tallahassee, FLA. *Democrat,* Sun., Mar. 5, 1972.

Recordings:

CRI SD 275.

Notes:

Compositional project for the Copley Award.

---

50   *Sonance*

Medium:

Carillon.

Movements:

Single movement, in seven sections, marked off with double bars and tempo changes (11').

Date:

2/25/64-3/13/64, NYC.

Final copy:

13 pp., ink on tissue.

Publication:

Published - special order - 11440534.

Dedication:

To Daniel Robins.

First Performance:

Wednesday, July 1, 1964, Rockefeller Memorial Chapel, University of Chicago. Daniel Robins, carillon.

Notes:

Commissioned by Daniel Robins for the Laura Spelman Rockefeller Memorial carillon. There are two ink-on-tissue versions: one version is labeled "for the Chicago carillon." The other version is labeled "concert pitch."

---

51 *Configurations*

Medium:

Fl., Pn..

Movements:

I-With intense gesture; II-With meditation; III-With joyous abandon (13' 30").

Date:

6/15/64-9/11/64, Chicago, Ill.

Final copy:

19 pp., ink on tissue.

Publication:

Published - special order - 114405990.

Dedication:

To Sue Ann Kahn.

First Performance:

Wed. Mar 23, 1966, Kaufman Auditorium, YM-YWHA, 92 St., New York City. Sue Ann Kahn, fl.; Robert Miller, pn.

Reviews and Articles:

(P) *The New York Times*, Thu., Mar. 24, 1966. *Buffalo Courier Express,* Wed., Jun. 11, 1980.

Recordings:

New World Records, NW 254.

---

52 *String Trio*

Medium:

Vln., Vla., Vcl.

Movements:

I-Molto legato e sonore; II-In a bravura cadenza-like manner:

sempre legato (13').

Date:

5/6/65-5/27/65.

Final copy:

18 pp., ink on tissue.

Publication:

Published - special order - 11440516S.

Dedication:

To the Kindler Foundation.

First Performance:

Monday, January 10, 1966, The Textile Museum, Washington, D.C. Allen Ohmes, vln.; William Preucil, vla.; Joel Krosnick, vcl.

Reviews and Articles:

The Washington Post, Wed., Jan. 5, 1966. (P) *The Washington Post,* Tues., Jan. 11, 1966. (P) *The Evening Star,* Washington, D.C., Tue., Jan. 11, 1966. *Chicago Tribune,* Tue., Mar. 8, 1988.

Notes:

Commissioned by the Kindler Foundation.

---

53 *Partita for Solo Violin*

Medium:

Vln.

Movements:

I-8th=60; II-8th=60; III-q=144 (16').

Date:

11/9/65 - 11/29/65.

Final copy:

14 pp., pencil on tissue.

Publication:

Published - special order - 114404820.

Dedication:

To Max Pollikoff.

First Performance:

Monday, January 30, 1967, Town Hall, New York City. Max Pollikoff, vln.

Notes:

Commissioned by the Koussevitzky Foundation.

---

54 *Poeme*

Medium:

Vla., Perc. (3 Toms, Bs. Dr., 3 Wd. Bl., 3 Irons, 2 Cymb., Lge Tam.)

Movements:

Single movement (11' 14").

Date:

1966.

Final copy:

15 pp., ink on tissue.

Publication:

Published - special order - 114405670.

Dedication:

To Rhoda Lee Rhea.

First Performance:

None (r.s.)

Notes:

Viola tunes C string down to B.

---

55 *Mutations II*

Medium:

Pn.

Movements:

Single movement in two sections:

I-Of majestic passion - of designs, movements, and forces - of majestic passion - of peace and quiet - of majestic passion - of majestic breadth; II-With furious wildness, intensity, brilliance and sound - of majestic passion - of majestic breadth (13' 30").

Date:

7/3/66-8/1/66.

Final copy:

15 pp., ink on tissue.

Publication:

Published - special order - 110406860.

Dedication:

Dedicated to Frances Burnett.

First Performance:

Wednesday, February 15, 1967, Bowling Green State University, Bowling Green, OH. Faculty Concert Series, Frances Burnett, pn.

Reviews and Articles:

Chicago Tribune, Mon., Apr. 17, 1976.

Notes:

Commissioned by Bowling Green State University.

---

56 *Partita for Violin and 13 Players*

Medium:

1.1.1.1 - 1.1.1.0, 2 Pc., Vln., Vla., Vc., Db.

Movements:

I-Adagio maestoso ("of Great Gesture"); II-Adagio delicatissimo ("of Simple Tenderness"; III-Adagio maestoso ("of Great Gesture"); IV-Moderato con brio ("of Happy Verve") (20').

Date:

1/5/66-8/30/66.

Final copy:

86 pp., ink on tissue.

Publication:

Rental - 0140480.

First Performance:

Thursday, January 26, 1967, Mandel Hall, University of Chicago. The Contemporary Chamber Players of The University of Chicago, Esther Glazer, vln.

Reviews and Articles:

Chicago Daily News, Thu., Jan. 26, 1967.

Notes:

Commissioned by the University of Chicago for its 75th Anniversary.

57   For Solo Trumpet

Medium:

Tpt.

Movements:

I-Legato sostenuto; II-Cadenza; III-Dolce, legato, delicatissimo (10′).

Date:

2/2/67–2/11/67, Chicago.

Final copy:

16 pp., ink on tissue.

Publication:

Published - special order - 114405620.

Dedication:

To Ronald Anderson.

First Performance:

(First American performance) Tuesday, March 25, 1969, Kaufman Auditorium, YM-YWHA, 92 St., New York City. Ronald Anderson, tpt.

Reviews and Articles:

(P) *The New York Times,* Wed., Mar. 26, 1969. *Mönchner Merkur,* Thu., Nov. 13, 1969.

Notes:

Also performed Friday, May 17, 1974, Carnegie Recital Hall. Ronald Anderson, tpt. The program notes read: "For Solo Trumpet will be performed tonight against the express wishes of the composer, who has placed a moratorium on all performances and on the availability of his music."

58   Partita-Fantasia for Cello and Sixteen Players

Medium:

2.2.2.2 - 1.1.1.0, 2 Pc., Vln., Vla., Db.

Movements:

I-Maestoso; II-Semplice; III-Cadenzas; IV-Rhythmic and joyous (20′).

Date:

3/11/67–7/23/67.

Final copy:

80 pp., ink on tissue.

Publication:

Rental - 0131036.

Dedication:

For the Serge Koussevitzky Music Foundation in the Library of Congress. Dedicated to the memory of Serge and Natalie Koussevitzky.

First Performance:

Friday, April 19, 1968, Mandel Hall, University of Chicago. The Contemporary Chamber Players of The University of Chicago, Joel Krosnick, vcl.

Reviews and Articles:

(P) *Chicago Tribune,* Sat. Apr. 20, 1968. *The New York Times,* Fri., Apr. 6, 1979.

59   Deux

Medium:

2 Pn..

Movements:

Single movement (4′ 41″).

Date:

7/18/67–7/30/67, Oxbow, MI.

Final copy:

18 pp., ink on tissue.

Publication:

Published - special order - 110406910.

Dedication:

To Philip Lorenze and Ema Bronstein.

First Performance:

Monday, April 14, 1969, Hall of the Americas, Pan-American Union, Washington D.C. Philip Lorenze and Ema Bronstein, pn.

Reviews and Articles:

(P) *The Evening Star* (Washington, DC), Tue. Apr. 15, 1969. (P) *The Washington Post,* Tue., Apr. 15, 1969. *The New York Times* Thu., Apr. 29, 1971.

60 *Three Concert Pieces for Young Players*

Medium:
Vln., Vla., Vcl., Pc.

Movements:
March; Song; Dance (no duration given).

Date:
7/30/67–8/1/67.

Final copy:
16 pp., engraved.

Publication:
Published - 114401680.

First Performance:
Unknown.

Notes:
Commissioned by The American String Teacher's Association (r.s.) On the ink-on-tissue title page: "University of Illinois String Project."

---

61 *Songs of Ecstasy for Soprano with Piano, Percussion and Tape*

Medium:
Sop., Pn., Pc., 2-track stereo tape.

Movements:
I-"Of One"; II-"Of Yes"; III-"My Beloved"; IV-"O Wonderful" (20').

Date:
8/30/67–9/30/67, Chicago.

Final copy:
47 pp., ink on tissue.

Publication:
Published - special order - 111401190.

Dedication:
To my wife, Vera.

First Performance:
Friday, May 23, 1969, Mandel Hall, University of Chicago. The Contemporary Chamber Players of The University of Chicago: Neva Pilgrim, sop; John Cobb, pn.; Rick Kvistad & Terry Appelbaum, pc.; Allan Schindler, tape.

Reviews and Articles:
Chicago Daily News, May 5, 1969. (P) *Chicago Today,* Sat., May 24, 1969. (P) *Chicago Tribune,* Sun., May 25, 1969. *Chicago Daily News,* Mon., May 26, 1969.

Notes:
Commissioned by the Fromm Foundation for Neva Pilgrim. Sources of text: Old Testament: Genesis. Walter Benton: "This Is My Beloved." Shakespeare: *As You Like It.* Joyce: *Ulysses.*

---

62 *Reyem (or Musical Offering for Flute, Violin, and Piano)*

Medium:
Fl., Vln., Pn.

Movements:
Single movement (6').

Date:
12/9/67–12/24/67.

Final copy:
13 pp., ink on tissue.

Publication:
Published - special order - 11440515S.

Dedication:
Dedicated to Leonard B. Meyer on his 50th Birthday.

First Performance:
Private performance at the University of Chicago for Leonard B. Meyer's fiftieth birthday (r.s.)

Notes:
"Reyem" is "Meyer" spelled backwards. Title on ink-on-tissue copy: "Reyem— a Musical Offering by Three (flute, violin, and piano)."

---

63 *Three Concert Pieces for Chamber Orchestra*

Medium:
Chamber Orchestra (r.s.)

Movements:
Unknown (r.s.)

Date:

Unknown (r.s.)

Final copy:

Cannot locate (r.s.)

Publication:

Not published.

Dedication:

None (r.s.)

First Performance:

Not performed (r.s.)

Notes:

Commissioned by the American String Teacher's Association.

---

64 *Praise (Oratorio for bass-baritone, double chorus, and chamber group)*

Medium:

2 Ob., 2 Tpt., 3 Tmb., 4 Pc., 2 Vln., Vla., Vcl., Db.

Movements:

I-Convocation; II-Invocation; III-Processional; IV-Interlude (54').

Date:

1971.

Final copy:

55 pp., ink on tissue.

Publication:

Rental - 0131038.

First Performance:

Saturday, February 28, 1976, Rockefeller Chapel, University of Chicago.

Reviews and Articles:

Chicago Sun Times, Sun., Feb. 22, 1976. (P) *Chicago Daily News,* Sat.-Sun., Feb. 28-29, 1976. Disc reviews: *Nevada State Journal,* Sun., Aug. 22, 1976. *Long Island Press,* Sun., Nov. 28, 1976. *Newsweek,* Mar. 7, 1977. *Los Angeles Times,* Sun., Oct. 22, 1978.

Recordings:

CRI SD 355.

Notes:

The February 28-29 premiere was Shapey's first new work to appear since 1969, when he declared a moratorium on all performances of his music "for personal and religious reasons." All performers are listed on the liner notes of the recording. Cello tunes C down to A. Source of text: Old Testament: Deuteronomy ("Hear O Israel" from the "Shema Israel" Jewish profession of faith).

---

65 *String Quartet No. 7*

Medium:

2 Vln., Vla., Vcl.

Movements:

I-Fantasy I, II, III, IV; II-Scherzando-leggiero; III-Largo-Largo, molto sostenuto et [sic] sonoro; IV-Passacaglia, maestoso (35' 54").

Date:

I-7/8/68, II-6/28/71, III-7/10/72, IV-10/21/72, Chicago.

Final copy:

68 pp., pencil on tissue.

Publication:

Published - special order- 114405740.

Dedication:

Commissioned by the Fromm Foundation. To Emanuel Zetlin.

First Performance:

Friday, April 22, 1977, Mandel Hall, University of Chicago. The String Quartet of The Contemporary Chamber Players of The University of Chicago: Elliot Golub & Everett Zlatoff-Mirsky, vln.; Lee Lane, vla.; Barbara Haffner, vcl.

Reviews and Articles:

(P) *Chicago Daily News,* Mon., Apr. 25, 1977. (P) *Chicago Tribune,* Mon., Apr. 25, 1977. Disc Review: *Stereo Review,* Sept., 1978. *Chattanooga Times,* Sun., Sept. 24, 1978. *American Record Guide,* Dec. 1978.

Recordings:

CRI SD 391.

66 Sonate No. 1 for Solo Violin

Medium:

Vln.

Movements:

I-Maestoso; II-Quasi march; III-Cantabile; IV-Rhythmic and brilliant (no duration given).

Date:

1972.

Final copy:

15 pp., pencil on tissue.

Publication:

Published - 41441151.

First Performance:

None.

Notes:

Footnote on first page of pencil-on-tissue score referring to opening measures: "taken from String Trio 1965; Kindler Foundation Commission, 2nd mvt."

67 Fromm Variations (31 Variations) for Piano

Medium:

Pn.

Movements:

Theme and thirty-one variations (c. 43-45′).

Date:

Begun 2/66, resumed 3/72, completed 1/28/73.

Final copy:

77 pp., pencil on tissue.

Publication:

Published - special order - 110406950.

Dedication:

Dedicated with love and admiration to Paul Fromm for his many years of personal friendship and generosity, and as the patron of twentieth-century music.

First Performance:

Thursday, May 17, 1979, Carnegie Recital Hall, New York City. Robert Black, pn.

Reviews and Articles:

The New York Times, Sat., Jan. 31, 1981, and Sun., Jun. 7, 1981. Disc reviews: *Fort Wayne News-Sentinel,* Sat., May 9, 1981. *Chattanooga Times,* Sat., Jun. 12, 1982. *St. Louis Globe Democrat,* Sat.-Sun., Dec. 20-21, 1980. *The Village Voice,* Jan. 21-27, 1981.

Recordings:

CRI SD 428.

68 O Jerusalem for Soprano and Flute

Medium:

Sop., Fl.

Movements:

I-(Broad, bel canto); II-My Name (With elan); III-Holy City (Amoroso); IV-Shalom Aleichem (10′ 40″).

Date:

1974.

Final copy:

8 pp., in two fold-out sheets, engraved.

Publication:

Published - 11140103.

First Performance:

Sunday, March 5, 1978, The Pittsburgh New Music Ensemble, Chatham College Theatre, Pittsburgh. Lynne Webber, sop.; David Tessmer, fl.; David Stock, cond.

Reviews and Articles:

(P) *Pittsburgh Post-Gazette,* Tue. Mar. 7, 1978. *The New York Times,* Wed., Jun. 11, 1988.

Recordings:

Opus One Recordings, Opus One 121.

Notes:

Begun in Israel during his first visit to that country, finished in Chicago, summer, 1974.

Notes:

There are several dates of completion of sections written in blue pencil throughout the score.

Source of text: The text of the entire work consists only of the words "O Jerusalem."

69 *Songs of Eros for Soprano, Symphony Orchestra, and Tape*

Medium:

3.3.3.3, A.Sax., T. Sax., Bar. Sax., 4.2.2.1, 6 Pc., Pn., Solo String Quartet, Str.

Movements:

Single movement (30′).

Date:

7/1/73–6/16/75, Chicago.

Final copy:

162 pp., pencil on tissue.

Publication:

Rental - 0110488.

First Performance:

None (r.s.)

Notes:

Sources of text: Old Testament: Song of Songs. Pierre Louys: "Songs of Bilitis". Joyce: *Ulysses*. Whitman: "Leaves of Grass."

---

70 *The Covenant for Soprano and 16 Players and Prerecorded Tapes*

Medium:

Fl., Ob., Cl., Bsn., Hn., Tpt., Tmb., Tb., 2 Pc., Pn., 2 Two-track stereo tapes, 2 Vln., Vla., Vcl., Db.

Movements:

I-It was; II-God of mercy; III-I believe; IV-It shall (45′).

Date:

7/15/77–8/23/77, MacDowell Colony, NH.

Final copy:

189 pp., pencil on tissue.

Publication:

Rental - 0131035.

Dedication:

Dedicated to Israel's 30th anniversary.

First Performance:

Friday, April 14, 1978, Mandel Hall, University of Chicago. The Contemporary Chamber Players of The University of Chicago, Elsa Charlston, sop.; Abraham Stokman, pn.

Reviews and Articles:

(P) *Chicago Tribune* and *Chicago Sun Times*, Mon., Apr. 21, 1978. *High Fidelity / Musical America,* Jul., 1978, vol. 28, no. 7 (MA p. 36). *The New York Times,* Sun., May 20, 1979. Disc review: *Chicago Tribune,* Dec. 12, 1982.

Recordings:

CRI SD 435.

Notes:

At the premiere performance, first movement Kaddish tape by Gershon Silin, second movement voice tape by Elsa Charlston. Sources of text: Nelly Sachs: "O, the Chimneys." Old Testament: Exodus, Isaiah. Walt Whitman: "Leaves of Grass." Pierre Louys: "Songs of Bilitis." Kadia Molodowski: *A Treasury of Yiddish Poetry*. Hayyim Bialik: *Modern Hebrew Poetry: Inscription on the Walls of a Cellar in Cologne, Jews Hiding from the Nazis.* Vera Klement: *Walking Upright* (Also see entry no. 29).

---

71 *Twenty-one Variations for Piano*

Medium:

Pn.

Movements:

Theme and twenty-one variations (c. 28′).

Date:

Begun 6/1/78–resumed 8/9/78–completed 8/29/78.

Final copy:

36 pp., engraved.

Publication:

Published - 41041230.

First Performance:

Saturday, January 20, 1979, Alice Tully Hall, Lincoln Center for the Performing Arts. Abraham Stokman, pn.

Reviews and Articles:

(P) *The New York Times,* Mon., Jan. 22, 1979.

Recordings:

CRI SD 496.

Notes:

Although not completely clear, I left the above dates (which are preceded by the words "begun - resumed - completed") exactly as Shapey wrote them on the final copy. Footnote on premiere program: "Written especially for Mr. Stokman."

72 *Trilogy (Song of Songs) I*

Medium:

Sop. 1.1.1.1 - 1.1.1.1, Pc., Pn., Four-track tape.

Movements:

Maestoso-largamento, 8th=44; I-8th=q=44; II-dotted q=8th=44; III-triplett q=q=66 Dolce (duration of entire Trilogy: 90′).

Date:

12/2/78-6/18/79.

Final copy:

192 pp., pencil on tissue.

Publication:

Rental - 0140484.

First Performance:

Saturday, April 30, 1980, Library of Congress, Washington, D.C. The Contemporary Chamber Players of The University of Chicago, Elsa Charlston, sop.; Ralph Shapey, cond.

Reviews and Articles:

(P) *The Washington Post*, Sat., Mar. 1, 1980. *Chicago Tribune,* Tue., Mar. 11, 1980. *Chicago Sun Times,* Tue., Mar. 11, 1980. Complete trilogy (I, II, III) review: *Musical America,* Aug., 1981, vol. 31, no. 8, p. 21.

Notes:

Commissioned by the Elizabeth Sprague Coolidge Foundation Commission from the Library of Congress. Source of text: Old Testament: Song of Songs (See also entry nos. 75 and 77: Song of Songs II and III).

73 *Evocation No. 2 for Cello, Percussion and Piano*

Medium:

Vcl., Pn., 4 pc. (Xyl., Glock., Woodbl., Cowbells, Timp., Toms, B. Dr., Sus. Cym., Tam.).

Movements:

I-Maestoso; II-Spiritoso; III-Cadenza, rubata bravura (18′).

Date:

6/22/79-7/7/79, Tanglewood.

Final copy:

36 pp., engraved.

Publication:

Published - 11440399P.

First Performance:

Tuesday, April 14, 1981, The Juilliard School, New York City. Joel Krosnick, vcl.; Gilbert Kalish, pn.; Gordon Gottlieb, James Baker, and Brian Slawson, pc.

Reviews and Articles:

(P) *The New York Times*, Thu., Apr. 16, 1981. The New York Times, Wed., Jan. 11, 1984.

Notes:

Commissioned by Joel Krosnick.

74 *Three for Six*

Medium:

Vln. (Vla.), Vcl., Fl. (Picc.), Cl (B. Cl.), Pc., Pn.

Movements:

I-Maestoso; II-Semplice, tenderly, cantabile; III-Maestoso vigaroso, Maestoso largamento (16′ 27″).

Date:

7/8/79-8/14/79, Tanglewood.

Final copy:

73 pp., ink on tissue (there is also an Ozolid copy of pencil on tissue).

Publication:

Rental - 11440552S.

Dedication:

Dedicated to Robert Black and the New York New Music Ensemble.

First Performance:

Sunday, January 25, 1981, Park School, Baltimore. New York New Music Ensemble: Jayne Rosenfield, fl.; Laura Flax, cl.; Curtis Macomber, vln.; Eric Bartlett, vcl.; Daniel Druckman, pc.; Alan Feinberg, pn.; Robert Black, cond.

Reviews and Articles:

(P) *The Sun Today* (Baltimore), Mon., Jan. 26, 1981. *The Boston Globe,* Tue., Feb. 20, 1990. *The New York Times,* Sun., Jun. 11, 1988. *San Francisco Chronicle,* Wed., Feb. 12, 1992.

Recordings:

CRI SD 509.

Notes:

Commissioned by the Chamber Music Society of Baltimore.

---

75 *Trilogy (Song of Songs) II*

Medium:

Bar., 1.1.1.1 - 1.1.1.1, Pc., Pn.

Movements:

I-8th=44 (triplett 8th=66); II-dotted 8th=66; III-q=60 (duration of entire Trilogy: 90′).

Date:

1/20/80-4/16/80, Chicago.

Final copy:

92 pp., pencil on tissue.

Publication:

Rental - 0140486.

First Performance:

Friday, April 24, 1981, Mandel Hall, University of Chicago. The Contemporary Chamber Players of The University of Chicago, Paul Kiesgen, bass.

Reviews and Articles:

(P) *Chicago Tribune*, Mon., Apr. 27, 1981.

Notes:

Cello tunes C down to A.

Source of text:

Old Testament: Song of Songs (See also entry nos. 72 and 77: Song of Songs I and III).

---

76 *Four Etudes for Violin*

Medium:

Vln.

Movements:

Four movements (r.s.), (8′ 22″) (r.s.)

Date:

1980

Final copy:

Could not locate (r.s.)

Publication:

Published - special order - 114406000.

Dedication:

None (r.s.)

First Performance:

None (r.s.)

Recordings:

Titanic (r.s.)

Notes:

Originally published by the American String Teacher's Association (r.s.).

---

77 *Trilogy (Song of Songs) III*

Medium:

Sop., Bar., 1.1.1.1 - 1.1.1.1, Pc., Pn., Two-track tape.

Movements:

Single movement (duration of entire Trilogy: 90′).

Date:

7/21/80-11/30/80.

Final copy:

100 pp., pencil on tissue.

Publication:

Rental - 0140488.

First Performance:

Friday, April 24, 1981, Mandel Hall, University of Chicago. The Contemporary Chamber Players of The University of Chicago, Elsa Charlston, sop.; Paul Kiesgen, bass.

Reviews and Articles:

(P) *Chicago Tribune*, Mon., Apr. 27, 1981.

Notes:

Cello tunes C down to A. Source of text: Old Testament: Song of Songs (See also entry nos. 72 and 75: Song of Songs I and II).

78   *Fanfares for Brass Quintet*

Medium:

2 C Tpt., Hn., Tmb., Tb.

Movements:

Single movement (3' 15").

Date:

1981.

Final copy:

6 pp., engraved.

Publication:

Published - 414402840.

First Performance:

Sunday, June 21, 1981, WFMT (= Chicago radio station) [Shapey's] 60th Birthday Concert. Contemporary Concerts, Inc., Chicago (r.s.)

Notes:

Commissioned by WFMT in celebration of their 30th birthday.

79*   *Evocation No. 3 for Viola and Piano*

Medium:

Vla., Pn.

Movements:

I-Passacaglia; II-Scherzo; III-Song (17' 09").

Date:

5/7/81-8/4/81.

Final copy:

22 pp., engraved.

Publication:

Published - 41441162.

First Performance:

Monday, October 18, 1982, Alice Tully Hall, Lincoln Center for the Performing Arts, New York City. Thomas Riebel, vla.; Susan Tomes, pn.

Reviews and Articles:

(P) *The New York Times*, Sun., Oct. 24, 1982. *Chicago Tribune*, Sun., Apr. 24, 1994.

Notes:

An asterisk to the right of the entry number indicates that the composition was generated by an organized collection of pitches Shapey has devised that he calls "The Mother Lode." This system is discussed in detail in Part II (page 65). Commissioned by the Naumburg Foundation for its International Viola Competition.

80* *Concerto Grosso for Woodwind Quintette*

Medium:

Fl., Bsn., Hn., Ob., Bb Cl.

Movements:

I-Tuttis; II-Solis; III-Scherzo (Quasi march); IV-Epilogue (12').

Date:

8/17/81-9/5/81.

Final copy:

24 pp., engraved.

Publication:

Score and parts published - 11440442.

Dedication:

Boehm Quintet.

First Performance:

Sunday, February 20, 1983, Guggenheim Museum Auditorium, New York City. The Boehm Quintet: Sheryl Henze, fl.; Phyllis Lanini, ob.; Don Stewart, cl.; Joseph Anderer, hn.; Robert Wagner, bsn.

Notes:

Commissioned by the Boehm Quintet.

81*   *Songs (for Soprano and Piano)*

Medium:

Sop., Pn.

Movements:

I-Dreams; II-Hope; III-Death (4′).

Date:

1982.

Final copy:

Cannot locate (r.s.)

Dedication:

Elsa Charlston.

Publication:

Not published.

First Performance:

November, 1982, Merkin Concert Hall, New York City. Elsa Charlston, sop.; Lambert Orkis, pn.

Reviews and Articles:

Chicago Tribune, Wed., Apr. 6, 1983.

Recordings:

Opus One Recordings, Opus One 106.

Notes:

Also scored for soprano, violin, clarinet, cello, and piano (entry no. 94). Sources of text for both works: E. A. Poe: "A Dream Within a Dream." Christina Rossetti: "Mirage." Arthur O'Shaugnessy: "Ode." Longfellow: "A Psalm of Life." Robt. Browning: "Easter Day." Pedrow Calderon de la Barca: "La Videas Sueno II." Old Testament: Genesis, Isaiah. John Bunyon: "The Pilgrim's Progress." Charles Leland: "Brand New Ballade: The Masher." Wordsworth: "Ode: Intimations of Mortality." Alice Meynell: "The Shepherdess." Wm. Morris: "The Wanderers." Shakespeare: *The Tempest, Anthony and Cleopatra.* Robt. Bridges: "I Love All Beauteous Things." P. B. Shelly: "The Indian Serenade." John Clare: "First Love." John Milton: "Paradise Lost." Owen Mert (E. R. B. Lytton): "Lucille." Oscar Wilde: "The Ballad of Reading Gaol." Wm. Walsh: "Song of All Torments." Alfred Lord Tennyson: "Lancelot and Elaine." Edward Young: "The Revenge." Algernon Charles Swinburne: "Atlanta in Calydon." E. B. Browning: "To George Sand: A Desire." Wm. Drummond: "Sonnet IX: Sleep, Silence Child." Rbt. Southey: "Carmen Nuptiale," "The Lay of the Laureate," "The Dream."

82*   *Passacaglia for Piano*

Medium:

Pn.

Movements:

Single movement in four sections labeled Maestoso, Appassionata, Exaltazione, Maestoso (13′).

Date:

1982.

Final copy:

14 pp., engraved.

Publication:

Published - 41041256.

Dedication:

Commissioned by and dedicated to Robert Black.

First Performance:

April, 1983, Abraham Goodman House, New York City. Robert Black, pn.

Reviews and Articles:

(P) *The New York Times,* Wed., Apr. 20, 1983.

Notes:

See entry no. 88.

83* Double Concerto for Violin, Cello, and Orchestra

Medium:
2.2.2.2 - 1.2.2.2, 5 Pc., Pn., Str.

Movements:
I-Maestoso; II-Maestoso; III-Vivace (31′ 30″).

Date:
7/25/82-12/29/82.

Final copy:
90 pp., ink on tissue.

Publication:
Rental - 0111219.

Dedication:
Dedicated to my Beloved.

First Performance:
Monday, January 23, 1984, The Juilliard School, New York City. Festival of Contemporary Music, Robert Mann, vln.; Joel Krosnick, vcl.; Juilliard Symphony, Ralph Shapey, cond.

Reviews and Articles:
(P) *The New York Times,* Thu., Jan. 26, 1984. (P) *New York,* Feb. 6, 1984.

Notes:
Commissioned by Joel Krosnick. Viola, cello, and double bass tune C down to A.

84* Discourse II

Medium:
Vln., Pn., Cl., Vcl.

Movements:
I-Maestoso; II-Brilliante; III-Delicato (15′ 46″).

Date:
4/10/83-5/16/83, Chicago.

Final copy:
55 pp., ink on tissue.

Publication:
Published - special order - 0160489.

Dedication:
Lewis Kaplan—Aeolian Players [sic].

First Performance:
Bolden College, ME (r.s.)

Notes:
Commissioned by Lewis Kaplan for the Aeolean Players. The duration given in the Presser catalogue of 7′ 13″ is incorrect. 7′ 13″ is the duration up to the end of a section on p. 32.

85* Fantasy

Medium:
Vln., Pn.

Movements:
I-Variatione (Theme and four variations); II-Scherzo; III-Cantabile, Delicato (11′ 53″).

Date:
5/24/83-6/4/83.

Final copy:
22 pp., ink on tissue.

Publication:
Published - special order - 114404660.

First Performance:
Monday, April 6, 1987, Merkin Concert Hall, New York City (r.s.)

Reviews and Articles:
Disc review: *Ovation,* May , 1987, vol. 8, no. 4, p. 62.

Recordings:
New World Records, NW 333.

Notes:
Commissioned by Eugene and Sylvia Gratovich.

86 Mann Duo for Violin and Viola

Medium:
Vln. (Vla.), Vla. (Vln.)

Movements:
I-Theme and variations (4); II - Song / tenero; III - Vivo; IV - Epilogue exaltazione (12′ 30″).

Date:
6/8/83.

Final copy:

11 pp., engraved.

Publication:

Published - 11440438.

Dedication:

Bobby and Nicholas Mann.

First Performance:

Thursday, January 12, 1984, Kaufman Auditorium, YM-YWHA, 92nd St., New York City. Robert Mann, vla.; Nicholas Mann, vln.

Reviews and Articles:

(P) *The New York Times*, Fri., Jan. 13, 1984.

Notes:

Page 1 of the final copy lists this work as the third work in a trilogy: I-Krosnick Soli (entry no. 87), II-Duo Variations (entry no. 100), III-Mann Duo for Violin and Viola. Viola and cello tune C strings down to A.

87*   *Krosnick Soli for Solo Cello*

Medium:

Vcl.

Movements:

Theme and ten variations (10′).

Date:

6/20/83-7/7/83.

Final copy:

10 pp., ink on tissue.

Publication:

Published (Presser) - 0160270. (Also see Notes below).

Dedication:

Dedicated to my dear friend Joel Krosnick and his wife Dinah.

First Performance:

Carnegie Recital Hall, New York City. Joel Krosnick, vcl. (r.s.)

Reviews and Articles:

The New York Times, Tue., May 7, 1996.

Notes:

Commissioned and published (engraved) by the American String Teacher's Association. Page 1 of the final copy lists this work as the first in a trilogy: I-Krosnick Soli, II- Duo Variations (entry no. 100), III- Mann Duo for Violin and Viola (entry no. 86). Cello tunes C down to A.

88*   *Passacaglia for Piano and Orchestra*

Medium:

Pn. and Orchestra (r.s.)

Movements:

Single movement (r.s.)

Date:

1983.

Final copy:

Cannot locate (r.s.)

Publication:

Not published.

Dedication:

None (r.s.)

First Performance:

None (r.s.)

Reviews and Articles:

None (r.s.)

Notes:

An "expanded" version of the Passacaglia for Piano (entry no. 82) (r.s.)

89*   *Gottlieb Duo for Piano and Percussion*

Medium:

Pn., Pc (3 Irons, 3 Woodbl., 5 Temple Bl., 3 Cym., Tam, 3 Toms, B. Dr., Glock.)

Movements:

I-Maestoso; II-Scherzo; III-Song (7′ 52″).

Date:

9/27/84-11/27/84, Chicago.

Final copy:

30 pp., ink on tissue.

Publication:

Published - special order - 114404650.

Dedication:

Commissioned by and dedicated to Gordon Gottlieb.

First Performance:

April 28, 1985, Merill Lynch Sunday Series, Quad City, MS. Gordon Gottlieb, pn.; Tuesday, March 31, 1987, Merkin Concert Hall, New York City. Gordon Gottlieb, pn. (r.s.)

90* *Psalm I For Soprano, Oboe, and Piano*

Medium:

Sop., Ob., Pn.

Movements: Prologue:

Prais'd Be; I-Sonore-Master of the Universe; II-Maestoso-Thy Covenant; III-Largamento-Day of Wrath; Epilogue-Exaltazione-O God! (7' 9").

Date:

10/29/84–12/8/84.

Final copy:

15 pp., ink on tissue.

Publication:

Published - special order - 111401170.

Dedication:

Dedicated to my very dear friend Henry Weinberg.

First Performance:

Saturday, January 17, 1987, Baltimore Museum of Art.

Reviews and Articles:

The Sun Today (Baltimore), Mon., Jan. 19, 1987 (r.s.)

Notes:

Sources of text: Whitman: "When Lilacs Last in the Dooryard Bloom'd." P. B. Shelly: "Prometheus Unbound." "Rebbe of Kotzk: The Promise" (trans. by Chaim Pottock). Henry Arthur Jones and Henry Hermon: "The Silver King" (see also entry no. 93).

91* *Groton Three Movements for Young Orchestra*

Medium:

Young Orchestra (r.s.)

Movements:

Three movements (r.s.)

Date:

1984.

Final copy:

Cannot locate (r.s.)

Publication:

Not published.

Dedication:

None (r.s.)

First Performance:

None (r.s.)

92* *Harmaxiemanda for Piano*

Medium:

Pn.

Movements:

Single movement (1' 30").

Date:

1984.

Final copy:

3 pp., engraved.

Publication:

Published - 11040677.

Dedication:

Wedding present to Carter Harman and Wanda Maximillian, Dear Friends.

First Performance:

(Date unknown), Rutgers University, Wanda Maxmillian, pn. (r.s.)

Reviews and Articles:

None (r.s.)

93*   *Psalm II*

Medium:

Sop., Ob., Vla., Vc., Db., Pn., Chorus.

Movements:

(8′).

Date:

1984.

Final copy:

Cannot locate (r.s.)

Publication:

Not published.

Dedication:

None (r.s.)

First Performance:

None (r.s.)

Notes:

Sources of text: Whitman: "When Lilacs Last in the Dooryard Bloom'd," P.B. Shelley: "Prometheus Unbound." "Rebbe of Kotzk: The Promise" (trans. by Chaim Potok. Henry Arthur Jones and Henry Hermon: "The Silver King" (see also entry no. 90).

94* *Songs No. 2 for Soprano and Four Instruments*

Medium:

Sop., Vln., Cl., Vcl., Pn.

Movements:

I-Beams; II-Hope; III-Death.

Date:

1984.

Final copy:

Information not available (r.s.)

Publication:

Not published.

Dedication:

None (r.s.)

First Performance:

None (r.s.)

Notes:

Same as Songs for Soprano and Piano (entry no. 81).

95*   *Tango Variations on a Tango Cantus for Piano*

Medium:

Pn.

Movements:

Single movement (no duration given) (r.s.)

Date:

1984.

Final copy:

Cannot locate (r.s.)

Publication:

Not published.

Dedication:

None (r.s.)

First Performance:

Thursday, February 27, 1986, DTW's Bessie Schoenberg Theater, New York City. Yvar Mikhashoff, pn. (r.s.)

96*   *Concertante No. I for Trumpet and Ten Players*

Medium:

Tpt. Solo, 1.1.1.1- 1.0.0.0, Pc., Str.

Movements:

I-Prologue; II-Song; III-Epilogue (10′ 30″).

Date:

Begun 8/8/80-resumed 7/18/84-completed 9/3/84.

Final copy:

46 pp., ink on tissue.

Publication:

Rental - 0140481.

Dedication:

Commissioned by and dedicated to Ronald K. Anderson.

First Performance:

Friday, April 24, 1987, Mandel Hall, University of Chicago. The Contemporary Chamber Players of The University of Chicago (featuring John

Bruce Yeh, cl.), Ronald Anderson, tpt., Ralph Shapey, cond.

Reviews and Articles:

(P) *Chicago Tribune,* Sun., Apr. 26, 1987.

Recordings:

New World Records, NW 355-2 (CD).

97*   *Variations for Organ*

Medium:

Org.

Movements:

Theme and six variations (18′).

Date:

3/12/85-3/24/85.

Final copy:

12 pp., engraved.

Publication:

Published - 11340036.

First Performance:

Monday, March 10, 1986, The Church of the Ascension, 5th Ave., New York City. David Schiller, org.

Reviews and Articles:

The New York Times, Sun., Mar. 2, 1986, and (P) Wed., Mar 12, 1986. *The Reader— Chicago's Free Weekly*—Fri., May 4, 1990.

Notes:

Commissioned by a grant from the National Endowment for the Arts by David Schiller, David Craighead, and Donald Sutherland.

98*   *Kroslish Sonate for Cello and Piano*

Medium:

Vcl., Pn.

Movements:

I-Maestoso; II-Delicato; III-Maestoso (22′).

Date:

3/27/85-4/6/85.

Final copy:

16 pp., engraved.

Publication:

Published - 11440457.

Dedication:

Dedicated to two dear friends, Joel Krosnick and Gilbert Kalish.

First Performance:

Wednesday, April 14, 1986, Harvard/Fromm Foundation Concert (location unknown) Joel Krosnick, vc.; Gilbert Kalish, pn. (r.s.)

Reviews and Articles:

(P) *The Boston Globe,* Thu., Apr. 15, 1986.

Recordings:

New World Records, NW 355-2 (CD).

Notes:

Footnote regarding the beginning of the first measure of the treble and bass piano staffs: "Taken from my Double Concerto" (entry no. 98). Cello tunes C down to A.

99*   *Symphonie Concertante*

Medium:

3.2.3.3 - 4.3.3.1, 2 Timp., 6 Pc., Pn., Vcl., Str.

Movements:

I-Maestoso, Brilliante; II-Scherzo (Vivo, Brilliante, Rhythmic) and Trio; III-Song: Cantabile (30′).

Date:

8/18/85.

Final copy:

82 pp., ink on tissue, copyist.

Publication:

Published - special order - 0111259.

Dedication:

The Philadelphia Orchestra.

First Performance:

Thursday, April 2, 1987, Philadelphia Academy of Music. The Philadelphia Orchestra, Ricardo Muti, cond.

Reviews and Articles:

(P) *The Philadelphia Enquirer,* Fri., Apr. 3, 1987. (P) *City Paper* (Philadelphia), Fri., Apr. 3–Fri., Apr. 10, 1987, issue No. 138. (P) *The New York Times*, Thu., Apr. 9, 1987. (P) *South Star* (Philadelphia), Thu., Apr. 9, 1987. (P) *Chestnut Hill Local* (Philadelphia), Thu., Apr. 9, 1987.

Notes:

Constitutional Commission underwritten by Johnson and Higgins Insurance Co., Phila.

100*   *Duo Variations for Violin and Cello*

Medium:

Vln., Vcl.

Movements:

Single movement, theme and variations (r.s.)

Date:

1985.

Final copy:

Cannot locate (r.s.)

Publication:

Not published.

Dedication:

Paul Zukovsky, Joel Krosnick.

First Performance:

None (r.s.)

Notes:

Page 1 of the final copy lists this work as the second work in a trilogy: I-Krosnick Soli (entry no. 87), II-Duo Variations, III- Mann Duo for Violin and Viola (entry no. 86). Cello tunes C down to A.

101*   *Mann Soli for Solo Violin*

Medium:

Vln.

Movements:

Single movement.

Date:

1985.

Final copy:

Cannot locate (r.s.)

Publication:

Not published.

Dedication:

Robert Mann.

First Performance:

None (r.s.)

102*   *Soli for Solo Percussion*

Medium:

1 Pc., three set-ups (A: 33 Glock, Wd. Bl., Irons, 4 Cymb., 4 Timp.; B: Toms, B. Dr., Vib., 4 Timp., 4 Tam.; C: Roto Toms, Temple Bl., Mar., Crot.) (r.s.) (See Notes.)

Movements:

Three movements (r.s.)

Date:

1985.

Notes:

Mvt. I is taped (A). Mvt. II he goes to B and plays against tape of A (Duet) Mvt. III he goes to C and plays against tape A & B (Trio) (r.s.)

Dedication:

Gordon Gottlieb.

First Performance:

Tuesday, January 26, 1993, Manhattan School of Music, New York City. New Music Consort; William Trigg, pc.; William Sigmund, sound engineer. (r.s.)

Publication:

Not published.

Final copy:

32 pp., ink on tissue.

103*   *Concerto for Cello, Piano, and String Orchestra*

Medium:

Vcl., Pn., Str.

Movements:

I-Prologue. Maestoso–variations; II- Psalm. Misterioso; III-Rondo. Spiritoso, gioioso–Epilogue. Maestoso (25′ 25″).

Date:

4/12/86-11/29/86, Chicago.

Final copy:

95 pp., ink on tissue.

Publication:

Rental - 416411300.

Dedication:

Dedicated to dear friends Joel Krosnick and Gil Kalish.

First Performance:

Monday, July 31, 1989, Tanglewood. The Boston Symphony, Joel Krosnick, vcl.; Gilbert Kalish, pn.

Reviews and Articles:

(P) *Los Angeles Herald Examiner,* Thu., Aug. 3, 1989. (P) *Newsday,* Mon., Aug. 7, 1989. (P) *The Village Voice,* Tue., Aug. 22, 1989. (P) *The Berkshire Eagle,* Fri., Aug. 4, 1989. (P) *The Boston Globe,* Wed., Aug. 2, 1989.

104*   *Songs of Love (I Am My Beloved's)*

Medium:

Sop., Pn.

Movements:

Two movements (r.s.)

Date:

1986.

Final copy:

Cannot locate.

Publication:

Not published.

Dedication:

Rondi Charlston (r.s.)

First Performance:

Monday, April 30, 1990, Carnegie Recital Hall, New York City. (r.s.)

Notes:

Sources of Text: Old Testament: Song of Songs. Gibran: *The Prophet.* Whitman: *Leaves of Grass.* These text sources are also used in Shapey's *Songs of Love (And My Beloved Is Mine)* (entry no. 105).

105* *Songs of Love (And My Beloved Is Mine)*

Medium:

Bar., Pn.

Movements:

Unknown (r.s.)

Date:

1986.

Final copy:

Cannot locate (r.s.)

Publication:

Not published.

Dedication:

None (r.s.)

First Performance:

None (r.s.)

Notes:

Sources of Text: Old Testament: Song of Songs. Gibran: *The Prophet.* Whitman: *Leaves of Grass.* These text sources are also used in Shapey's *Songs of Love (I Am My Beloved's)* (entry no. 104).

106*   *In Memoriam for Soprano, Baritone, and Nine Players*

Medium:

Sop., Bar., 1.1.1.1 - Hn., 2 Vln., Vla., Vcl.

Movements:

Single movement (no duration given).

Date:

7/7/87-7/17/87.

Final copy:

49 pp., ink on tissue, copyist.

Publication:

Rental - 0050009.

Dedication:

For my dear friend, Paul Fromm, 1906-1987.

First Performance:

Sunday, October 4, 1987, Mandel Hall, University of Chicago (performers unknown) (r.s.)

Reviews and Articles:

None (r.s.)

Notes:

Sources of text: Old Testament: Psalms 121 and 23 (Kaddish).

107*   *Theme Plus Ten for Harpsichord*

Medium:

Hpschd.

Movements:

Theme and ten variations (c.12′).

Date:

Chicago 3/21/87, Aspen, Colorado 7/27/87-8/3/87.

Final copy:

14 pp., engraved.

Publication:

Published - 41041288.

Dedication:

Commissioned by and dedicated to Bob Conant.

First Performance:

October (day unknown), 1987, Skidmore College, Saratoga Springs, NY. Bob Conant, hpschd. (r.s.)

Reviews and Articles:

Daily News Gazette (Schenectedy, NY) (r.s.)

Notes:

Suggestions for harpsichord registration are provided by Robert Conant in a preface to the published score.

108*   *Concertante No. II*

Medium:

Alto Sax solo, 1 (Picc., B. Fl.). 1 (E.Hn.). 1 (Eb Cl., B.Cl.).1 (B. Bsn.) - 1.1 (Picc. Tpt.). 1 (B. Tmb.)., 3 Pc., Solo Str. (Vl. II doubles Vla.)

Movements:

I-Variations; II-Rondo scherzo; III-Passacaglia (21′ 5″).

Date:

7/4/87-10/8/87.

Final copy:

94 pp., ink on tissue, copyist.

Publication:

Rental - 0030852.

Dedication:

NEA and Cynthia Sikes.

First Performance:

Friday, April 21, 1989, Mandel Hall, University of Chicago. The Contemporary Chamber Players of The University of Chicago (featuring Cynthia Sykes, alt. sax.), Ralph Shapey, cond.

Reviews and Articles:

Chicago Sun Times, Sun., Apr. 16, 1989. (P)
Chicago Tribune, Sun., Apr. 23, 1989.

Notes:

Cello and contra bass tune C string down to A.

109*   *Songs of Joy for Soprano and Piano*

Medium:

Sop., Pn.

Movements:

I-Maestoso; II-Leggiero, Rhythmic; III-Allegro, Gioia (9′ 4″).

Date:

10/9/87-10/18/87.

Final copy:

20 pp., pencil on tissue.

Publication:

Published - special order - 111401140.

Dedication:

To my dear Elsa Anniversary gift (10/12/87).

First Performance:

Saturday, March 11, 1989, WFMT (=FM radio station, Chicago), Elsa Charlston, sop.; Erik Weimer, pn. (r.s.)

Notes:

Sources of text: Keats: "Endymion, Ode To Melancholy." Old Testament: Isaiah. Rbt. Browning: "Saul." Milton: "The Passion." Thomas Hardy: "The Darkling Thrush." Shakespeare: Sonnets. Southey: "Thalia the Destroyer." Schiller: "An Die Freude." Blake: "Infant Joy" (r.s.: All of the above taken from the *Oxford Dictionary of Quotations,* 3rd ed. (1979), Angela Partington, ed., Oxford University Press Inc., NY.)

110*   *Variations On A Cantus for Piano*

Medium:

Pn.

Movements:

Theme and five variations (6′).

Date:

10/21/87-10/25/87.

Final copy:

8 pp., engraved.

Publication:

Published - 11040681.

Dedication:

Dedicated to my dear friend Shulamit (=Shulamit Ran) on her birthday, October 21, 1987, and Get Well, October 20, 1987.

First Performance:

None (r.s.)

Reviews and Articles:

None (r.s.)

111*   *Variations for Viola and Nine Players*

Medium:

Solo Vla., Fl. (Picc., Bs. Fl.), Eb Cl., Cl. (A Cl.), Bs. Cl., Pc., Pn.

Movements:

I-Variations; II-Scherzo; III-Chant. (no duration given).

Date:

1/5/86-11/5/88.

Final copy:

71 pp., ink on tissue, copyist.

Publication:

Rental - 0150494.

Dedication:

Walter Trampler.

First Performance:

Friday, April 20, 1990, Mandel Hall, University of Chicago. The Contemporary Chamber Players of The University of Chicago (featuring Walter Trampler, vla.), Ralph Shapey, cond.

Reviews and Articles:

(P) *Chicago Tribune,* Mon., Apr. 23, 1990.

112*   *Songs of Life*

Medium:

Sop., Vcl., Pn.

Movements:

Three movements, listing not available (r.s.).

Date:

1988.

Final copy:

59 pp., ink on tissue.

Publication:

Not published.

Dedication:

Library of Congress.

First Performance:

Thursday, February 28, 1991-March 1, 1991, Washington D.C. 70th Birthday Concert (r.s.)

Reviews and Articles:

The Chicago Sun Times and the *Chicago Tribune,* Tue., Apr. 4, 1995

Notes:

Commissioned by the Elizabeth Sprague Coolidge Foundation in the Library of Congress. Sources of text:Whitman: *Leaves of Grass*. Edmond Rostand: "La Princess Lointaine." Shakespeare: *Timon of Athens*. Oscar Wilde: *A Woman of No Importance*. Longfellow: "Resignation." Thomas Osbert Mordaunt: "Verses Written During the War." Henry James: "Letter to H. G. Wells." Julian Grenfell: "Into Battle." P. B. Shelley: "Adonais." All of the above taken from the *Oxford Dictionary of Quotations,* 3rd ed. (1979), Angela Partington, ed., Oxford University Press Inc., NY.

113*   *Thanks to the Human Heart for Soprano and Piano*

Medium:

Sop., Pn.

Movements:

Unknown (r.s.)

Date:

1988.

Final copy:

Cannot locate (r.s.)

Publication:

Not published.

Dedication:

Ellen T. Harris (r.s.)

First Performance:

None (r.s.)

114   *Two for One for Solo Snare Drum*

Medium:

1 Sn. Dr.

Movements:

Two movements (4' 30").

Date:

9/30/88–10/1/88.

Final copy:

4 pp., copyist.

Publication:

Smith publications.

Dedication:

Stuart Saunders Smith.

First Performance:

None (r.s.)

Notes:

Published as part of a four-volume set of works for solo snare entitled *The Noble Snare: Compositions for Unaccompanied Snare Drum In Four Volumes.* Shapey's "Two For One" is in volume four.

115*   *Concerto Fantastique for Symphony Orchestra*

Medium:

3.3.3.3 - 4.4.4.1., 12 Timp., 8 Pc., Str.

Movements:

I-Variations, Maestoso; II-Elegie to Paul Fromm, Largo; III-Intermezzo— Homage to the Chicago Symphony Orchestra, Cantabile; IV-Rondo—To The Chicago Symphony Orchestra, Maestoso (53' 38").

Date:

1/10/88–9/8/89.

Final copy:

150 pp., ink on tissue, copyist.

Publication:

Published - special order - 0111366.

Dedication:

Chicago Symphony Orchestra.

First Performance:

Thursday, November 21, 1991, Mandel Hall, University of Chicago. Chicago Symphony Orchestra, Ralph Shapey, cond.

Reviews and Articles:

The University of Chicago Chronicle, Thu., Nov. 7, 1991. *Chicago Tribune,* Sun., Nov. 10, 1991, Tue., Nov. 12, 1991. *Chicago Sun Times,* Sun., Nov. 17, 1991. *Chicago Tribune,* Tue., Nov. 19, 1991. *Chicago Daily Herald,* Thu., Nov. 21, 1991. (P) *Chicago Sun Times,* Fri., Nov. 22, 1991. (P) *Chicago Tribune,* Fri., Nov. 22, 1991.

Notes:

Commissioned by the Chicago Symphony Orchestra for the University of Chicago and the Chicago Symphony Orchestra Centennial. Written under date on last page of ms: "God HELP ME!"

116   *Soli for Percussion Duo*

Medium:

2 Pc. (Pecussionist A: Timp., Roto Toms, Glock., Xyl., Mar., Wd. Bl., Toms, Cymb., Chimes. Percussionist B: Timp., Roto Toms, Crot., Vib., Dulcimer, Sn., B. Dr., Tams, Chimes.)

Movements:

Single movement (20').

Date:

1989.

Final copy:

54 pp., ink on tissue.

Publication:

Not published.

Dedication:

Erik Charlston and Gordon Gottlieb.

First Performance:

Friday, April 19, 1991, Fromm Concert, Chicago (r.s.).

117*   *Intermezzo for Dulcimer and Keyboards*

Medium:

Dulcimer, Pn., Celeste. (r.s.)

Movements:

Single movement (r.s.) (no duration given).

Date:

1990.

Final copy:

17 pp., ink on tissue. (r.s.)

Publication:

Not published.

Dedication:

Collins Trier.

First Performance:

Sunday, January 26, 1992, Mandel Hall, University of Chicago. Shapey 70th Birthday Celebration Concert (r.s.), Collins Trier, dulcimer.

Reviews and Articles:

(P) *Chicago Tribune,* Tue., Jan. 28, 1992.

118*   *Centennial Celebration for Soprano, Mezzo Soprano, Tenor, Bass, and Twelve Players*

Medium:

Sop., M-Sop., Ten., Bar., Chorus, Fl., A. Fl., Ob., Eng. Hn., Cl., B. Cl., Bsn., B. Bsn. C Tpt., Bb Picc. Tpt., Hn., 2 Vln., Vla., Vcl., Db.

Movements:

Introduction; I-Choral Chant; II- Dedication; III-In Memory; IV-Prayer of Thanksgiving (no duration given).

Date:

12/1/90-5/31/91.

Final copy:

93 pp., ink on tissue (r.s.).

Publication:

Not published.

Dedication:

Dedicated to the University of Chicago.

First Performance:

Sunday, January 26, 1992, Mandel Hall, University of Chicago. Shapey 70th Birthday Celebration Concert (r.s.)

Reviews and Articles:

Chicago Tribune, Tue., Jan. 28, 1992.

Notes:

Sources of Text: Old Testament: Psalm 148. Wm. Wordsworth: "The Excursions," "Character of the Happy Warriors." P. B. Shelley: "The Witch of Atlas." Henry Vaughan: "They Are All Gone." Donne: "The Legacy." W. S. Gilbert: "Iolanthe." Catullus:" Carmina." (r.s.: All of the above taken from the *Oxford Dictionary of Quotations,* 3rd ed. (1979), Angela Partington, ed., Oxford University Press Inc., N.). Bernard O. Brown (Dean, Rockefeller Memorial Chapel): Excerpts from the Rockefeller Memorial Chapel Service of Dedication, 10/2/88.

119* *Movement of Varied Moments for Two*

Medium:

Fl., Vib.

Movements:

Single movement (7′).

Date:

10/28/91–11/06/91.

Final copy:

10 pp., Copyist

Publication:

Smith Publications.

First Performance:

Tuesday, March 3, 1992, University of Akron, Akron, OH (r.s.).

Reviews and Articles:

None (r.s.).

Notes:

In celebration of the opening of the Sylvia Smith archives, University of Akron, March, 3, 1992.

120* *Trio 1992*

Movements:

Three movements (r.s.)

Medium:

Vln., Vcl., Pn.

Date:

1992.

Final copy:

45 pp., ink on tissue, copyist.

Publication:

Published - special order - 114406670.

Dedication:

Joel Krosnick, Gilbert Kalish, and Joel Smirnoff.

First Performance:

Sunday March 7, 1993, Miller Hall, Columbia University, New York City. Joel Smirnoff, vln.; Joel Krosnick, vcl.; Gilbert Kalish, pn.

121* *Evocation No. 4*

Medium:

Vln., Vcl., Pn.

Movements:

I-Prologue and Duet No. 1, Prologue No. 2, Duet No. 2, Prologue No. 3, Duet No. 3, Prologue No. 4, Duet No. 4, Solo No. 1, Prologue no. 5, Solo No. 2; II-Prologue No. 1 and Trio No. 1, Trio No. 2, Trio No. 3, Epilogue - Coda; III-Scherzo - Rondo, Coda, Epilogue, Prologue, Solo.

Date:

1994.

Final copy:

62 pp., ink on tissue.

Dedication:

For my dear friends:

Gilbert Kalish, Joel Krosnick, Joel Smirnoff, and Bill Trigg.

First Performance:

Sunday, April 23, 1995, Miller Hall, Columbia University, New York City. Joel Smirnoff, vln.; Joel Krosnick, vcl.; William Trigg, Pc.

Reviews and Articles:

(P) *The New York Times,* Wed., April 26, 1995. *The New York Times,* Tue., May 7, 1996.

Publication:

Published - special order - 114-40808

122* *Inventions*

Medium:

Cl., Pc.

Movements:

I-Elegante, vivo, misterioso; II-Rondo/scherzo - con brio; III-Misterioso.

Date:

1992.

Final copy:

40 pp., ink on tissue.

Dedication:

To Ed Gilmore, Thanks for his Town Hall, NYC concert for my seventieth birthday.

First Performance:

Friday, April 23, 1993, Mandel Hall, University of Chicago. The Contemporary Chamber Players of The University of Chicago. Edward Gilmore, cl., Douglas Waddell, pc.

Reviews and Articles:

(P) *Chicago Tribune,* Mon., Apr. 26, 1993.

Publication:

Published (in preparation as of July 5, 1996) - 114-4040

123* *Lullaby*

Medium:

Sop.; Fl.

Movements:

I-Dolce (2' 30").

Date:

1992.

Final copy:

2 pp., computer copied.

Dedication:

To our two grandchildren (Rosetta Teweles Shapey, born Jan. 12, 1992, and Miles Calman Shapey, born Nov. 23, 1993), Love, Ralph Shapey and Elsa Charlston.

First Performance:

Friday, April 22, 1994, Mandel Hall, University of Chicago. Joan Heller, sop., Mary Stolper, fl.

Reviews and Articles:

(P) *Chicago Sun Times,* Mon., Apr. 25, 1994. *Chicago Tribune,* Sun., Apr. 24, 1994.

Publication:

Published - 111-40151

124* *Rhapsody*

Medium:

Vcl., Pn.

Movements:

I-Bravuro - Giocoso - Bravuro, Bravuro - Appassionate, quasi dance - Bravuro (ad lib cadenza) - Maestoso, exaltazione.

Date:

1993.

Final copy:

20 pp., ink on tissue.

Dedication:

Chanukah gift to two wonderful friends: Joel Krosnick and Gilbert Kalish.

First Performance:

Friday, Aug. 4, 1995, Composer's Conference, Wellesley College, Wellesley, MA. Joel Krosnick, vcl., Gilbert Kalish, pn.

Publication:

Published - special order - 114-40738

125* *String Quartet No. 8.*

Medium:

2 Vln., Vla., Vcl.

Movements:

I-Prologue and Six Fantasias; II- Scherzando - Trio; III-Bel canto (17' 9").

Date:

1993.

Final copy:

21 pp., Computer Copied.

Dedication:

To the Ying String Quartet.

First Performance:

Tuesday, October 25, 1994, Alice Tully Hall, Lincoln Center, New York, The Ying String Quartet: Timothy and Janet Ying, vln.; Phillip Ying, vla.; David Ying, vcl.

Reviews and Articles:

(P) *The New York Times,* Thu., Oct. 27, 1994. *The Boston Globe,* Wed., Aug. 16, 1995. *The Berkshire Eagle,* Wed., Aug. 16, 1995.

Publication:

Published - special order - 114-40777.

Notes:

Commissioned by the Naumberg Foundation, 1993, for the Ying String Quartet

---

126*   *String Quartet No. 9.*

Medium:

2 Vln., Vla., Vcl.

Movements:

I-Introduction - Five Variations - Exaltations - Maestoso; II-Scherzo - Trio; III-Canzonetta; IV-Rondo - Fu'gue - Maestoso (21' 30").

Date:

1995.

Final copy:

10 pp., Computer copied.

First Performance:

May 4, 1996, Madison, Wisconsin, The Pro Arte Quartet.

Reviews and Articles:

(P) *Isthmus,* Fri., May 10, 1996.

Publication:

Published - special order - 114-40819.

Notes:

Commissioned for the Pro Arte Quartet by the University of Wisconsin, Madison School of Music, for their one hundredth anniversary.

127*   *Trio Concertante*

Medium:

Vln., Pn., Pc.

Movements:

I-Four Variations; II-Chaconne; III- Rondo (ca. 14' 30").

Date:

1992.

Final copy:

53 pp., ink on tissue.

Dedication:

To Willard Edward Abel and Ronald Sidney Shapey.

First Performance:

April 24, 1994, San Francisco, Abel Steinberg Winant Trio.

Reviews and Articles:

San Francisco Chronicle, Wed., April 27, 1994.

Publication:

Published - special order - 114-40839.

Notes:

Commissioned by the Abel - Steinberg - Winant Trio.

128*   *Dinosaur Annex*

Medium:

Vln., Glock., Vib., Mar.

Movements:

I-Maestoso - Bel Canto - Vivo - Scherzando - Semplice, sostenuto - Maestoso (3).

Date:

1993.

Final copy:

8 pp., computer copied.

Dedication:

Dinosaur Annex, for their fiftieth anniversary (1944-1995).

First Performance:

Oct. 30, 1994, First And Second Church, Boston, Mass.

Reviews and Articles:

(P) *The Boston Globe,* Tue., Nov. 1, 1994. *Chicago Sun Times,* Tue., Apr. 4, 1995.

Publication:

Published - special order - 114-40736.

129* Constellations

Medium:

Cl., B. Cl., T. Sax., Vcl., Elect. Gui., Elect. Bass Gui., Pn., Pc.

Movements:

I-Prologue - Four Fantasies; II-Dolce; III-Scherzando - Trio - Coda; IV-Epilogue, impomente - Coda, exaltation (22').

Date:

1993.

Final copy:

36 pp., computer copied.

Dedication:

To Bang On A Can All Stars.

First Performance:

May 8, 1994, Alice Tully Hall, New York, Bang On A Can All Stars, R. Shapey, cond.

Reviews and Articles:

(P) *The New York Times,* Wed., May 11, 1994. *The Chicago Tribune,* Tue., Apr. 4, 1995.

Publication:

Rental.

130* Sonata Appassionata.

Medium:

Vcl., Pn.

Movements:

I-Maestoso, appassionata - Elegante, cantabile - Imposing - Joyful, dance-like - Appassionata; II-Minuet - Scherzo - Gently - Trio - Coda; III-Rondo, maestoso, appassionata - vigoroso, verve, rhythmic - Energico - Vibrant, imposing, appassionata - Vigoroso, verve, rhythmic - Maestoso, appassionata.

Date:

1995.

Final copy:

42 pp., computer copied.

Dedication:

To my dear wife, Elsa Charlston and dear friends Gilbert Kalish and Joel Krosnick.

First Performance:

Performance scheduled for 1997.

131* Discourse Encore

Medium:

Vln., Cl., Vcl., Pn.

Movements:

I-Bravuro - Vigoroso, rhythmic - Dolce, cantabile - Bravuro - Coda, maestoso.

Date:

1996.

Final copy:

11 pp., computer copied.

Dedication:

To the Aeollean players for my seventy-fifth Birth year.

First Performance:

Saturday, July 27, 1996, Charles E. Gamper Festival of Contemporary Music, Seventy-Fifth Birthday Celebration in honor of Ralph Shapey.

132* Goethe Songs

Medium:

Sop., Pn.

Movements:

I-1, Spirit - Cantabile; 2, The Song - Leggierro - Giocoso; 3, Tree - Life - Appassionata; 4, Peace Gone - Maestoso; 5, Dee - Glory - Solenne; 6, Woman - Cantabile; II-1, Master - Bravura, Spiritoso, Vibrant; 2, Poetry - Life - Vibrant, vigoroso; 3, Bredd - Sorrow - solenne; 4, Light - Appasionata, largamente, imponent; 5, Peace - Dolce, cantabile; 6, Beloved - maestoso, appasionata, exaltazione.

Date:

1995.

Final copy:

20 pp., computer copied.

Dedication:

To my wife Elsa Charlston for our tenth anniversary.

Notes:

(r.s.: Source of text: The *Oxford Dictionary of Quotations,* 3rd ed. (1979), Angela Partington, ed., Oxford University Press Inc., NY.)

133*   *Sonata Profundo*

Medium:

Pn.

Movements:

I-Introduction - Maestoso, Six Variations - Coda; II-Scherzando - Trio - Coda; III-Serenade; IV-Rondo (18′).

Date:

1995.

Final copy:

31 pp., computer copied.

Dedication:

To Russell (Buddy) Sherman.

First Performance:

Scheduled for January 17, 1997, Boston, Mass.

Notes:

Commissioned by Russell Sherman. At the end of the piece, Shapey wrote: "Go, Buddy, Go, in a Voice of Thunder." On the check sent to Shapey, Mr. Sherman wrote "The Voice of Thunder."

134*   *Stony Brook Concerto*

Medium:

Picc./Fl., Ob., Cl., Bsn., Hn., Tpt., B. Tmb., 2 Pc., Vln., Vcl., Pno.

Movements:

I-Bel canto, Dolce - Maestoso, largamente - Rhythmic, joyous, spiritoso - Brilliante, bravura - Sostenuto, cantabile, sonorous - Cantabile, Elegante - Maestoso, exaltazione; II- Scherzo - Rhythmic, vigoroso, joyous, trio - Coda; III-Dedicated to the memory of Dr. Joan Greenstone, beloved daughter of Paul and Erika Fromm), Introduction - Funeral March, elegy - maestoso, exaltazione (14′).

Date:

1996.

Final copy:

58 pp., computer copied.

Dedication:

To Stony Brook State University for my seventy-fifth birth year.

First Performance:

Scheduled for Tuesday, November 26, 1997, Staller Center, Stony Brook State University, Ralph Shapey, cond.

SHAPEY'S COMPOSITIONAL METHOD

SHAPEY'S COMPOSITIONAL METHOD

The Mother Lode

It seems appropriate to include in this catalogue an explanation of "The Mother Lode," the method that Shapey has been using in all of his compositions since 1981, beginning with his *Evocation No. 3* (Entry No. 79) for Viola and Piano. That is, Shapey's last forty-one consecutive works were written from a single row and its associated simultaneities and (often) rhythms. Furthermore, he shows no signs of discontinuing his use of it. Only three works written since 1981 are not based on the Mother Lode. All three are for unpitched percussion instruments: *Soli for Solo Percussion* (entry no. 102), *Two for One for Solo Snare Drum* (Entry no. 114), and *Soli for Percussion Duo* (entry no. 116).

This explanation presents the "Mother Lode," briefly explains its anatomy, and points out its presence in the openings of an assortment of Shapey's works. It is neither an analysis nor a critical evaluation of the method.

Shapey's Structures Worksheet (The "Mother Lode")

Example 1 is Shapey's Mother Lode. On this worksheet, the prime of a twelve-note row—labeled P_0-1-12 is on the bottom staff.[1] Shapey frequently uses this row, or some transformation of it, as a cantus firmus. Its retrograde-labeled R_0-1-12 is on the top staff.[2] A series of "assigned aggregates" (the term Shapey applies to the pitches between prime and retrograde) appears on the middle staffs.[3]

Below that is a rhythm, which Shapey tells us is "the cantus rhythm." Shapey explains: "There's not much to say about this rhythm except that it is the rhythm of the cantus that I thought up from the beginning. I have A and B so I can switch around. I put it down as something I might use. I might have used it religiously early on. But basically, sometimes I use it, sometimes I choose not to."[4]

---

[1] When asked why two rows of numbers—1–12 and 12–1—appear below the worksheet, Shapey replied "Sometimes I'm using the retrograde pitches above as well as the pitches of the prime below. Having both sets of numbers on the bottom makes for easy reading" (telephone conversation with Ralph Shapey, February, 1993).

[2] This discussion duplicates Shapey's idiosyncratic labeling. That is, P_0-1 is the first pitch of the untransposed row/cantus firmus, and so on. R_0-12 refers to the same pitch as P_0-12. The designation R_0, then, informs the reader that the retrograde is in operation. Thus, in any given transposition, the numbers 1–12 always represent the same pitch classes. P_1-1-12 indicates that the row is transposed up a semitone, and so on.

[3] Some of the pitches (mostly in the retrograde) are written several leger lines above the treble staff. I originally recopied Shapey's worksheet placing these pitches an octave lower and added an octave sign. When I showed my copy to Shapey, he requested that I recopy the worksheet exactly as he sent it to me. His reason: "I'm a violinist. I wrote them up there because I'm comfortable in that register; I think in that register. And when I compose, I tend to use those pitches in that register" (telephone conversation, March, 1992).

[4] Telephone conversation with Ralph Shapey, February, 1993.

Let us first examine the row. Notice that if we reversed the two adjacent pitches B and G so that the first hexachord reads F♯, D, E♭, A, G, B, the two hexachords of the row would be inversionally equivalent. Presenting the row as Shapey does results in eight consecutive semitone-related simultaneities between the prime and its simultaneously occurring retrograde pitch (R₀-10-3).

Shapey explains that in constructing the Mother Lode, he saw to it that each simultaneity "would include at least one interval of a third, a fifth, and a tritone."[5] Apparently, Shapey considers the intervals with 3, 4, 8, and 9 semitones as "thirds" and the intervals with 5 and 7 semitones as "fifths." Shapey states that, in addition to the inclusion of a third, fifth, and tritone, yet another criterion for the construction of the Mother Lode was that certain simultaneities should be related to each other by common tones to allow for smooth voice leading in chord progressions.[6]

Example 1. Shapey's worksheet (the "Mother Lode").

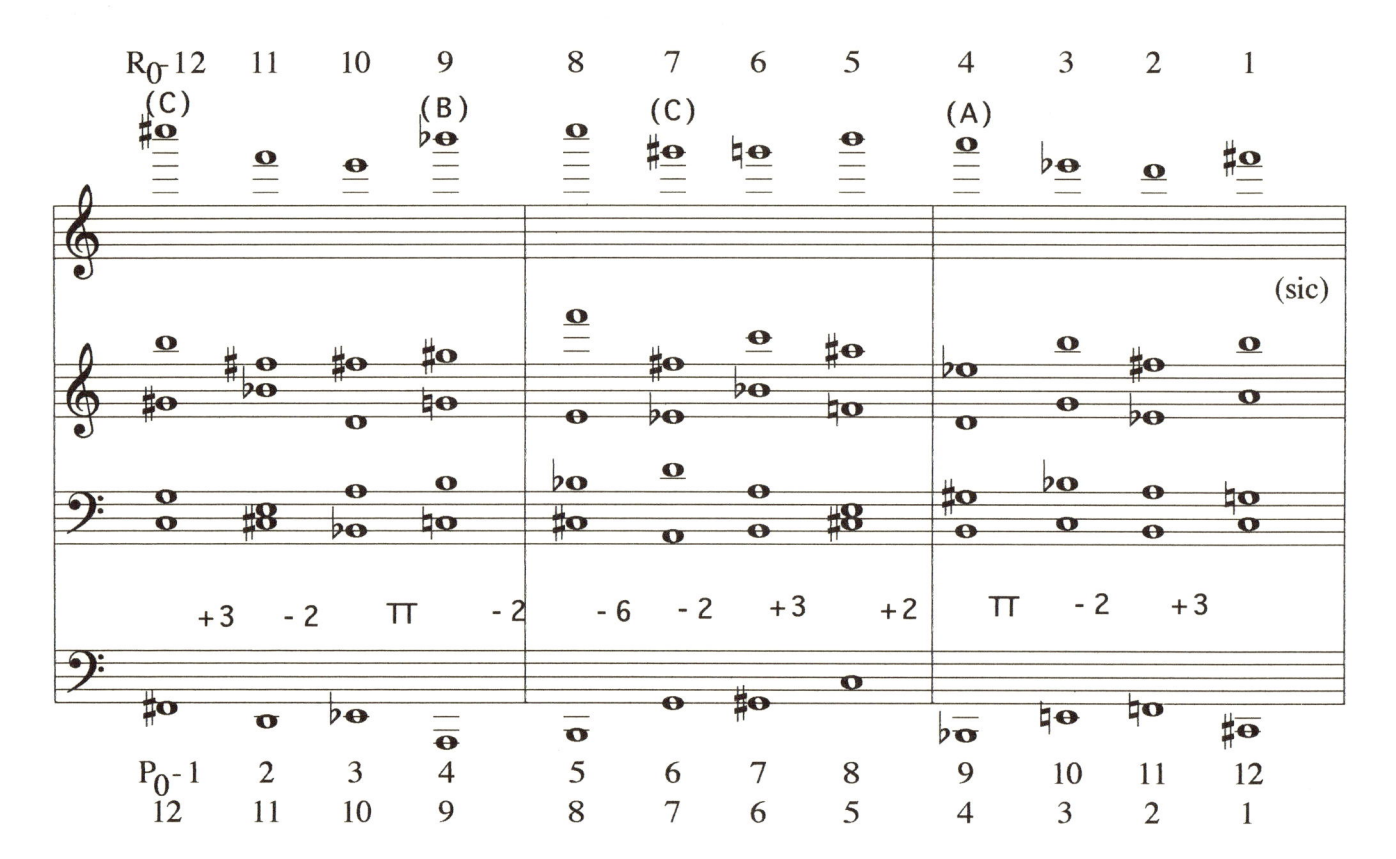

---

[5]Telephone conversation with Ralph Shapey, June, 1992.

[6]Telephone conversation with Ralph Shapey, March, 1992

THE MOTHER LODE

67

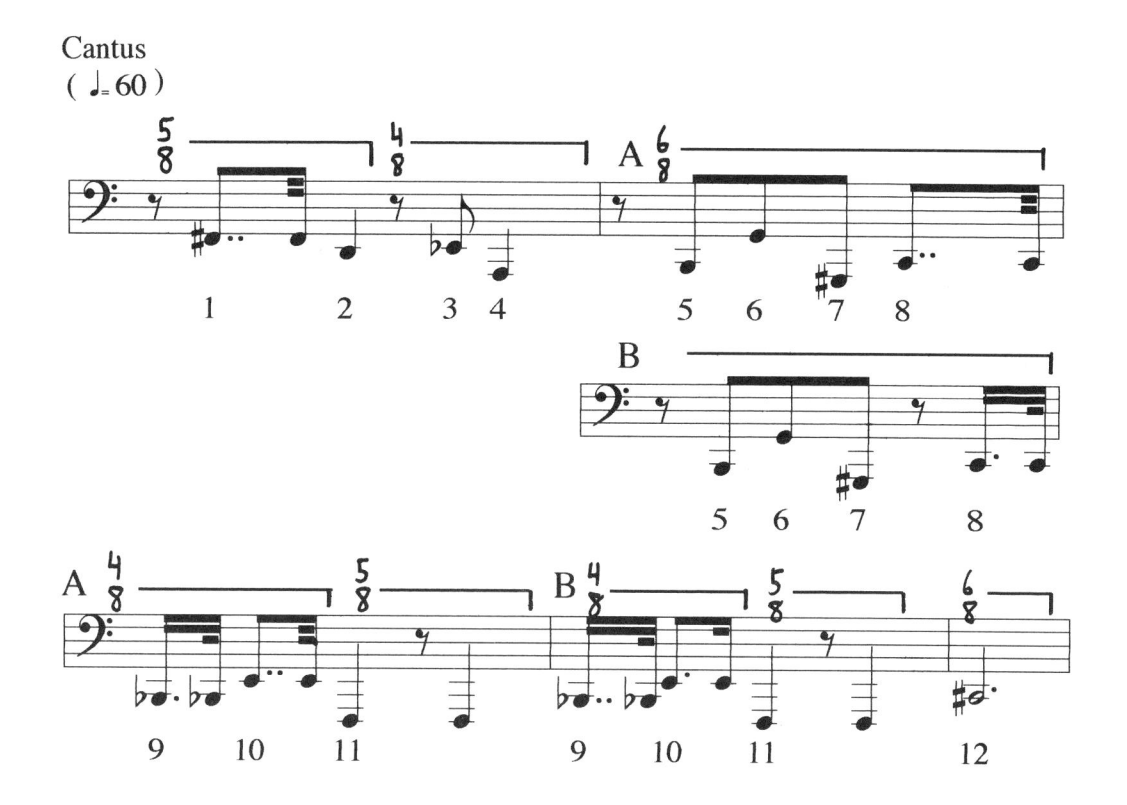

[Musical example: Cantus (♩=60), bass clef, showing order numbers 1-12 across multiple measures with time signature changes (5/8, 4/8, 6/8, etc.) and labeled sections A and B]

In example 1, we can see that the "assigned aggregates"[7] of P_0-5 and 8 have the same pitch classes, that [P_0-1 and 4 have A♭, C, G, and B in common], that the aggregates of P_0-1 and 12 differ only by one pitch (A♭ in P_0-1, A in P_0-12), and so on. The relationship of the aggregates of P_0-1 and 12 is especially significant. That these two order numbers differ by only one pitch means that the passage from the end of the unfolding of the row and its simultaneities to the beginning of the next unfolding can be exceptionally smooth. At the same time, the fact that P_0-1 and P_0-12 aggregates differ by one pitch means that the completion of any given unfolding of the row will not be one of total return to the opening sonority.

The Mother Lode can be described yet another way: it includes many adjacencies of segments of the row. In the example below, the "Mother Lode" is shown with those pitches circled that are verticalized consecutive order numbers in P_0; the order numbers are listed above each simultaneity.

---

[7]Hereto and after I will refer to the "assigned aggregates" as aggregates.

Example 2. Mother Lode with circled adjacencies.

For example, the consecutive vertical aggregate pitches of P_0-1 include P_0-5, 6, 7, 8; the vertical assigned aggregate pitches of P_0-2 include P_0-9, 10, 11, 12; the vertical aggregate pitches of P_0-3 include P_0-4, 5, 6, 7, 8, 9.

The uncircled pitches (that is, those which are not part of the vertical consecutive order numbers) of P_0-1-3 and 5-8 have a relationship with each other that is similar to the intervals prominent in the row. Each simultaneity in the Mother Lode includes the intervals of a fifth, a third, and a tritone. The uncircled pitches of P_0-1-3 make up three dyads of a fifth (F♯-C♯), a third (D-F♯), and a tritone (B♭-E), the very same intervals. In the group of order numbers and aggregates from P_0-5-8, there are four uncircled pitches which comprise a pair of thirds (B-G, and G♯-B). The "assigned aggregates," then, are directly derived from the row itself, which consists mostly of thirds (P_0-1-2, 5-6, 7-8, 11-12), plus two tritones (P_0-3-4, 9-10) and two fifths (the relationship between P_0-1 and 12).

The openings of five selected works which employ the Mother Lode are discussed below. The choice of openings as opposed to some other segment of a work was not completely arbitrary; it seemed best to observe the unfolding of the Mother Lode in parallel contexts, over a brief span, and in different works selected from early, middle, and recent Mother Lode compositions.

Analyses

Entry No. 79: Evocation No. 3 for Viola and Piano (1981) (Score on p. 75)
I. Passacaglia[8]

The viola presents P_0-1-12 in bars 1-3. In bars 2-3 the row unfolds in the piano in the bass as a passacaglia-like theme in dotted eighths. In bars 2-3, on the first of the two bass staffs in the piano, also in dotted eighths, are twelve dyads of assigned aggregates (C-G, C#-E, B♭-A, and so on) copied exactly from the Mother Lode worksheet, third staff down. Finally, on the treble staff in the piano, twelve trichords of aggregates occur, copied exactly from the top two staffs of the Mother Lode worksheet. These include the retrograde as the top pitch, treated as an equal member of the assigned aggregates.

The row begins again in bar 4, in augmented and slightly varied rhythms, and arrives on P_0-12 at a cadence at the end of bar 10. Above this the viola, beginning on the last beat of bar 3, presents first the order numbers P_0-1-4. Then a series of assigned aggregate collections in an unordered series occurs—sometimes as rolled chords, sometimes linearly—with the retrograde treated as an equal member of the assigned aggregates. That is, aggregate 1 (C-G#-B) occurs in bar 4 as a rolled chord with an aggregate 1 pitch as the first pitch in the melodic line that follows. This melodic line consists of the pitches of aggregates 2, 11, 1, 5, 6, and 8 (circled in the score). In bar 7 the unfolding of the Mother Lode in the viola continues with aggregate 1 (or 12), 8, and 11 over passacaglia pitches G# and C (P_0-7 and 8) in the bass. In bar 8, above P_0-9 (B♭) in the bass, the viola unfolds aggregate 1 (or 12) as a rolled chord, followed by the pitches of aggregate 8 (E, F, C#, and B♭ at the beginning of bar 8). Bar 8 continues with three pitches of aggregate 11 (B, A, E♭), then aggregate 1 (or 12) as a rolled chord with B♭ as its uppermost pitch (possibly a doubling of P_0-9). In bar 9 and 10 in the bass the last three pitches of the passacaglia occur (E, F, C#) above which is the unfolding of aggregates 3 and 1 in bar 9, and P_0-1-4 at the cadence in bar 10. The third phrase (bars 11-12) repeats bars 2-3.

In the fourth phrase (bars 13-18) the piano consists solely of a series of twenty-four quintuplets, each introduced by a sixteenth rest. The five-note simultaneities at the beginning of each quintuplet consist of aggregates 1-12 in bars 13-16 and repetitions of bar 13 in bars 17 and 18. Also in the piano in bars 13-18, the linear pitches that follow each unfolding, for example, in bar 5 (C-F#, D, E♭, A) are generated in three ways. The first quintuplet in bar 13 is an unfolding of P_0-1-4 (F#, D, E♭, A). The second quintuplet in that bar is made up of the pitches of aggregate 2 (G-C#) plus three pitches "borrowed." from aggregate 10. The third and fourth quintuplet are an unfolding of pitches with the same intervals as those of the unfolding of P_0-1-4, i.e., the intervals 4, 1, 6.

Bar 14 repeats bar 13. Bars 15 and 16 in the piano unfold aggregates 5-12 which occur as a series of eight simultaneities at the beginning of each of the eight quintuplets. The linear pitches, again, are generated by the intervals of P_0-1-4 (4, 1, 6). Finally, as the viola cadences in bars 17 and 18 where the piano presents two consecutive repetitions of bar 13. In bars 17 and 18, the pitches in the viola include two pitches from aggregate 4 (G#-B) and three pitches from aggregate 5 (G, F, C#, the latter of which is also the cadential P_0-12).

---

[8]In this work Shapey omits bar lines in several places on the score. For easier reference dotted bar lines and measure numbers where changes of meter occur have been added by the author.

Entry No. 87: Krosnick Soli (1983)
(Score on p. 78)

Below is a series of twelve four-note simultaneities which Shapey has extracted from the Mother Lode and which appear as grace note chords on page two of the working copy of his score. It is from these simultaneities, along with the row (which Shapey excludes from his sketch of the grace note simultaneities) that Shapey has constructed his Krosnick Soli. Shapey says that he extracted four-note simultaneities because he was working with a four-stringed instrument.[9]

Example 3. Grace note simultaneities extracted from the Mother Lode.

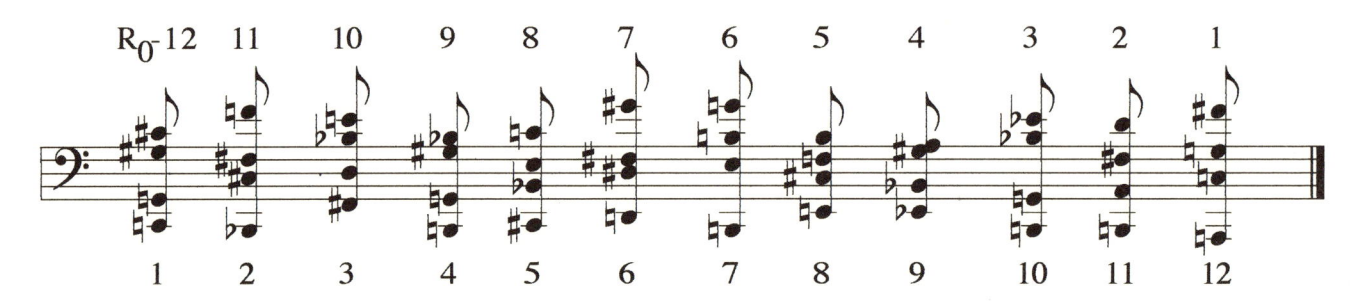

Shapey explains that his only criterion for the selection of these "grace note simultaneities" was their sound.[10] In this altered collection, Shapey has kept the retrograde order numbers as the top pitches. In addition, Shapey has made two alterations in the "grace note simultaneities." All of them were made by excluding one pitch from the Mother Lode with two exceptions: grace note simultaneities 7 and 9. Grace note simultaneity 7 excludes three pitches (C, A, B♭), doubles the B, and includes an E which Shapey says he "borrowed" from aggregate 8.[11] Grace note simultaneity 9 is the only simultaneity which contains its corresponding order number-P_0-9 (B♭)-from the row/cantus firmus.

SECTION I

The *Krosnick Soli* consists of a theme and variations in eleven sections labeled simply I to X, with a Coda. Shapey explains that he regards each variation as a solo piece, hence his use of the Italian plural, *Soli*.

In bars 1–6, the row appears in the bass as a cantus firmus/passacaglia theme. Above this the assigned aggregates appear as arpeggiated figures with the retrograde occurring simultaneously above it. Again, Shapey says he presents the Prime and Retrograde in this fashion often in his music.[12] Actually, he does this in all five of the pieces discussed here. The retrograde in the top voice is treated in this section as an equal member of the aggregates. Also, in this opening section, Shapey withholds use of the bottom pitch of each "grace note simultaneity;" they will appear in the next section.

---

[9]Telephone conversation with Ralph Shapey, March, 1992.
[10]Ibid.
[11]"Borrowing" is the term Shapey uses to describe a procedure he employs often in his music. For example, because P_0-3 (E♭) has as its simultaneous retrograde pitch R_0-10 (E), Shapey perceives a relationship between assigned aggregates 3 and 10. Therefore, when he is employing the order number or aggregates of P_0-3 he feels free to "borrow" one or more pitches from P_0-10. Shapey says he does this "all the time" in his music. (Telephone conversation with Ralph Shapey, March, 1992.)

[12]Telephone conversation with Ralph Shapey, August, 1989.

The work begins with stern, double-dotted figures, above which are heard briskly rolled trichords reminiscent of the Bach suites for solo cello. Indeed, Shapey instructs the player to "break chords (as in Bach) bottom to top and back to bottom held notes."[13] In addition, Shapey employs scordatura, tuning the first string down from C to A.

SECTION II

Section II (bars 7–15) is the first variation. Here the row and aggregates unfold over nine bars through ten ascending arpeggiations. The simultaneous retrograde, heard as the highest pitches in the rolled chords in section I, is absent. The lowest members of the grace note simultaneities which were omitted from section I have now been added: C in bar 7, B♭ in bar 8, F♯ in bar 9, and so on.

While the pitches of the row in Section I were unfolded in the bass as a quasi-passacaglia theme, the pitches of the row in Section II appear in the uppermost voice, usually as points of arrival of the ascending arpeggiated aggregates. The shifting of emphasis from bass to soprano is assisted by assigning dotted rhythms to the highest register and by the absence of a downbeat at the beginning of each upward-sweeping quintuplet.

In bar 7 aggregate 1 is followed by P_0-1 and 2. In bar 8, aggregate 2 is followed by P_0-3, 4, and 5. Aggregates 3 and 4 unfold in bar 9, aggregate 5 unfolds in bar 10, followed in the same bar by P_0-6 and 7. Bar 11 begins with aggregate 6 followed by a repeat of P_0-4 (so labeled because this A belongs to no neighboring aggregate) and aggregate 7. Bar 12 consists of P_0-8, 9, and 10 followed by three pitches from aggregate 8.

Bar 13 is introduced by aggregate 9 with B natural instead of B♭ as one of the aggregate pitches. Possibly this is "borrowed" from aggregate 10 which follows. P_0-11 occurs at the end of bar 13. Bar 14 consists of aggregate 11 followed by P_0-11, bar 15 consists of aggregate 12 followed by P_0-12.

---

[13]Shapey, Ralph. *Krosnick Soli for Solo Cello*, p. 1.

Entry No. 90: Psalm I for Soprano, Oboe, and Piano (1984)
(Score on p. 79)

PROLOGUE

In the Prologue (bars 1–6) the soprano and oboe simultaneously unfold the prime of P_0 in the cantus rhythm (example 1) and the retrograde, almost in first species counterpoint. This simultaneous unfolding of prime and retrograde recurs in all of the works selected for this discussion. Shapey states that he does this often in his music.[14]

SECTION I

In section I ("Master of the Universe"), each instrument operates independently, unfolding the row and/or its assigned aggregates. In the soprano line, the pitches from aggregate 1 (G♯, C♯, G, C, F♯) begin in bar 8, followed by pitches from aggregate 2 (the overlapping F♯, then F, B♭, E) in bar 9, followed by the pitches of aggregate 3 (the overlapping E, then E♭, A, D, B♭, F♯), and so on. The score is marked to show that aggregates 4, 5, 6, 7, and 8 unfold from bar 9 to the cadence in bar 17. As the soprano phrase draws to its close in bars 13–14 (with the text "O God, O God"), the opening motive F♯-D (i.e., P_0-1-2) recurs. These two pitches are derived from the currently unfolding aggregate 6. It should also be noted that in the soprano part the order numbers—both prime and retrograde—are treated as equal members of the assigned aggregates (R_0-12 in bar 8, then P_0-1, R_0-3, and P_0-3 in bar 9, etc.) This is not always the case in Shapey's Mother Lode works.

In the first phrase (bars 7–14), the oboe enters in bar 7 and the soprano enters in bar 8 in strict imitation, though some soprano pitches are in different registers.[15] The only exception is the addition of aggregate-pitch E in the oboe in bar 11.

Along with this oboe-soprano imitation, the piano unfolds the prime, retrograde, and aggregates. The piano part consists of arpeggiated sixteenth notes followed by dotted figures. Shapey selects aggregates 3–12 to unfold in bars 7–13 and aggregates 1–12 to unfold in bars 14–18. At the same time, the dotted figures at the end of each arpeggiation contain the retrograde of the row in the upper register and the prime in the lower register. P_0-1-12 and R_0-12-1 each unfold once, simultaneously, in bars 7–13. From bar 14 to the cadence in bar 18, aggregates 1–12 unfold once again, this time with the order numbers treated as equal members of the aggregates. After the cadence on the downbeat of bar 18, there is a closing statement where the soprano and oboe repeat the opening (bars 1–7).

In this work, as in others discussed here, the unfolding of the row delineates the structure. The arrival at P_0-12 or its aggregate (or the arrival on R_0-1, if the retrograde is unfolding) coincides with cadences and ends of sections.

---

[14]Telephone conversation with Ralph Shapey, August, 1989.

[15]There is an error in bar 12 in the soprano. "The G underneath the word a in the passage 'show me *a* sign' is supposed to be an E" (telephone conversation with Ralph Shapey, March, 1993).

Entry No. 107: Theme Plus Ten (1987)
(score on p. 84)

THEME

The theme (bars 1-13) consists of the unfolding of P_0-1-12 as a cantus firmus in octaves in the bass, and the unfolding of aggregates 1-12 above it. In these aggregates both prime and retrograde order numbers are included as equal members (order numbers labeled). The unfolding of P_0-1-12 delineates the structure of the opening theme (for the cadence at the end of the opening theme coincides with the arrival of P_0-12). In addition, each order number and its corresponding aggregate is confined to a single measure and each measure changes meter.

The aggregates unfold in a pattern. They are written as a series of repeating dyads, sometimes in the same register, usually in a different register, often inverted, and appearing as a series of "voice crossings," as indicated in the score. Bar 1 is typical of the rest of the section, and of the next two variations as well. For example, the dyad C-F# on the third beat in the treble staff occurs inverted on the fourth beat of the bass staff. The C#-G# on the second beat of the bass staff occurs inverted on the treble staff (the dyads are circled in the score).

VARIATION I

Variation I (bars 14-26) consists of twelve arpeggiations of the twelve aggregates unfolding over thirteen bars of alternating 3/4 and 3/8 meter. The order numbers occur in both the right hand and left hand in octaves and are interspersed with the aggregates (for example, in bars 14-19 the pattern is: aggregate 1, P_0-1-2, aggregate 2-3, P_0-3-4, aggregate 4-5, P_0-5-6, and so on). As in bars 1-13, prime and retrograde order numbers occur not only in octaves but as equal members of the aggregates, distributed through the arpeggiations. Also as in bars 1-13, each of the twelve aggregates is combined with prime and retrograde order numbers as equal members of the aggregates. A Complete set of the twelve aggregates and order numbers are confined to a single bar as dyads in various registers, and often in "voice crossings" within each bar (circled and connected by a dotted line in bars 1-16).

VARIATION II

Variation II (bars 27-39) is less contrapuntal and more rhythmically direct than variation I. The twelve order numbers occur as downbeats in each of the thirteen bars (the last two bars contain P_0-12), while the aggregates occur as a series of tetrachords in a repeating double-dotted rhythm. Once again, order numbers appear as equal members of the aggregates and individual pitches and dyads occur in frequent voice crossings throughout the variation.

Entry No. 102: Concertante No. 2 for alto saxophone and fourteen players (1987)
(Score on p. 87)

I. VARIATIONS

In *Concertante No. 2* all twelve order numbers plus the retrograde and the assigned aggregates unfold in the opening phrase (bars 1–5). The complete row (P_0-1-12) occurs, in unison, in the bass trombone and double bass in the cantus rhythm. In the solo saxophone P_0-1-7 unfolds in the first bar (in a different rhythm from the cantus), P_0-1-6 recurs in the second bar, then P_0-7-12 unfolds in the third bar, and P_0-8-12 in the fourth and fifth bars. Likewise, in the piccolo trumpet R_0-12-1 unfold over bars 1–5. Finally, in the remaining wind instruments (piccolo, oboe, E♭ clarinet, bassoon, and horn) aggregates 1–12 unfold as simultaneities over bars 1–5.

In the second section (bars 6–15) an ostinato consisting of P_0-1, 2, 3, 4 - 9, 10, 11, 12 recurs ten times in roto toms and timpani as a series of dotted eighth notes. This is joined in bar 6 by various percussion instruments of indefinite pitch. In bar 9 the cello simultaneously unfolds R_0-12, 11, 9, 10 - 3, 4, 2, 1 in identical rhythm to the roto toms. The cello repeats these pitches, in the same order, in bar 13.

Beginning in bar 8 the saxophone presents a series of arpeggiations made up of the assigned aggregates and certain pitches derived from the row. Aggregates 1 - 4 unfold in bar 8. Note that in bar 8 the pitches of aggregate 4 (F-C♯-B♭-E) are also P_0-5, 6, 7, 8, which are "missing" from the ostinato in timpani and roto toms.

In the context of P_0, R_0, and its aggregates Shapey also includes fragments of the row, as in bar 9 in the saxophone where Shapey unfolds seven pitches: C♯, A, B♭, E, F♯, D, D♯. Shapey describes these pitches as derived from the intervals of P_0-1-7 (i.e., the intervals 8, 1, 6, 2, 8, 1). Such transpositions of segments of the row occur "all the time" in his music.[16] Also in bar 9 the cello enters and unfolds, in identical rhythm, the pitches of the roto toms: P_0-12, 11, 9, 10, and P_0-1, 2, 3, 4. These four pitches could also be in the Retrograde. The cello re-enters in bar 11 with a reordering of the same eight pitches: order numbers 12, 11, 9, 10, and P_0-1, 2, 3, 4. At the next entry of the cello in bar 13, these pitches occur as P_0-1, 2, 3, 4 - 9, 10, 11, 12. Finally, in bar 15, they recur as R_0-12, 11, 10, 9 - 4, 3, 2, 1 with P_0-1 (C♯) as a cadential pitch.

In bar 10 the saxophone unfolds aggregates 5, 6, and 5 again. This is imitated in the trumpet in bar 11. Also in bar 11 the saxophone repeats the pitches of bar 9 (C♯, A, B♭, E, F#, D, D#) as the trumpet plays the pitches of the saxophone from bar 10 (E, C, F, C♯, etc.). In bar 12, the saxophone unfolds aggregates 9, 10, and 11, that are repeated in bar 13 by the trumpet. At the same time in bar 13, the saxophone continues with a transposition of P_0-8-12: G, F, B, C, C♯. In bar 14, the saxophone first plays a C,[17] then unfolds aggregates 11 and 12. Finally, in bar 15, the saxophone repeats its pitches from bar 13 as the trumpet unfolds aggregate 12.

---

[16]Telephone conversation with Ralph Shapey, February, 1993.

[17]This pitch is neither borrowed nor retained from the previous aggregate. Two likely possibilities are that Shapey considers this C an anticipation of the C in the following agg 12, or that it is P_0-8.

APPENDIX A

Evocation No. 3
for Viola and Piano

Duration: c. 16'30"

RALPH SHAPEY
(1981)

I. Passacaglia

① Viola plays from score.
② Comma equals a short breath pause.
③ Irrational rhythms: play as sight picture.

© 1985 by Theodore Presser Co., Bryn Mawr, Pa.
414-41162

All Rights Reserved
Printed in U.S.A.

International Copyright Secured

Unauthorized copying, arranging, adapting or recording is an infringement of copyright. Infringers are liable under the law.

① A medium breath pause.

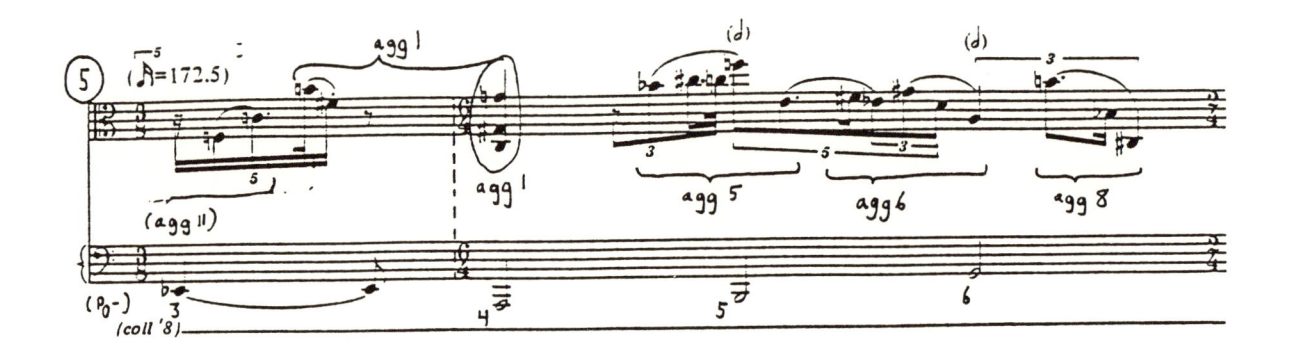

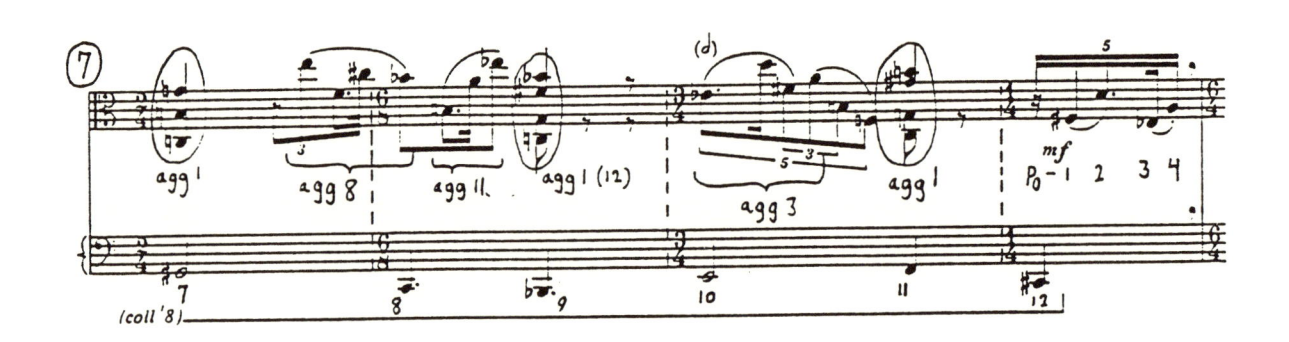

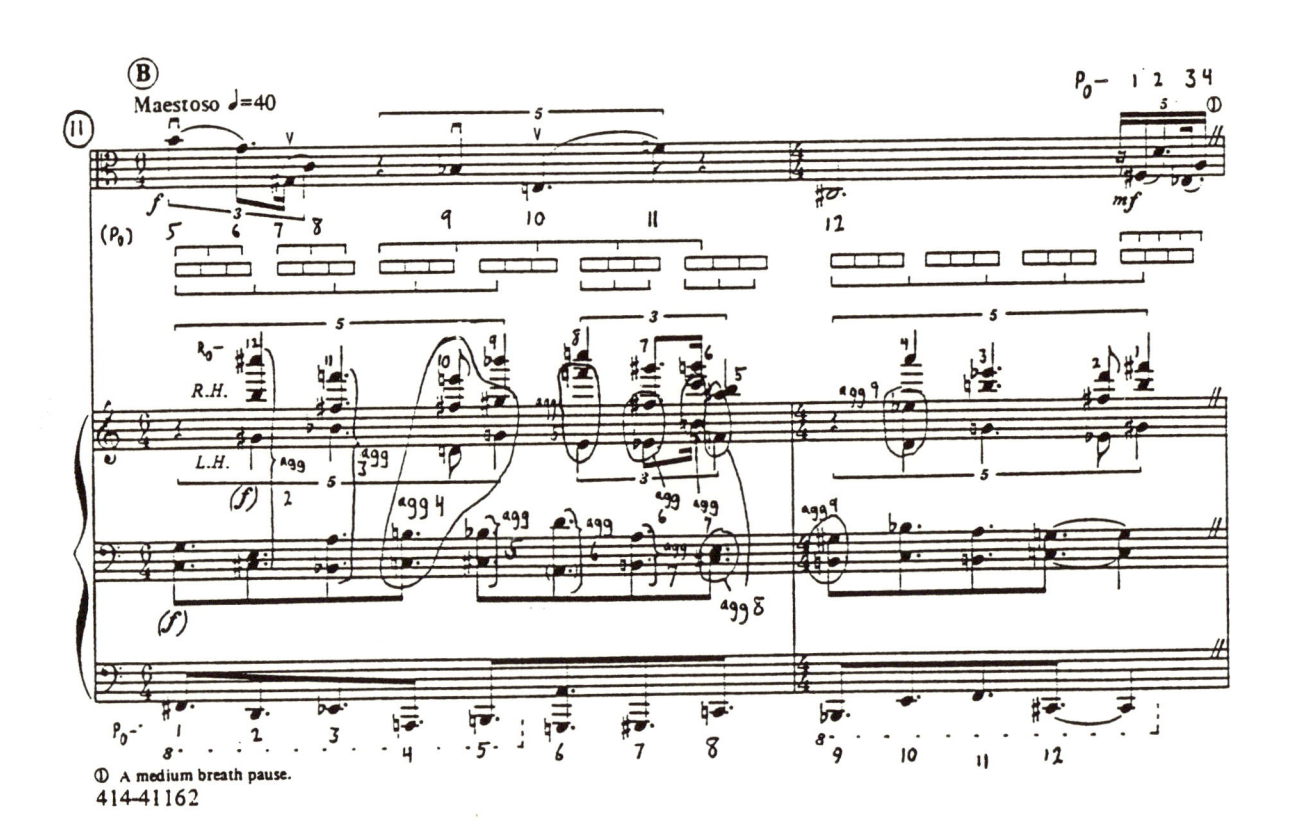

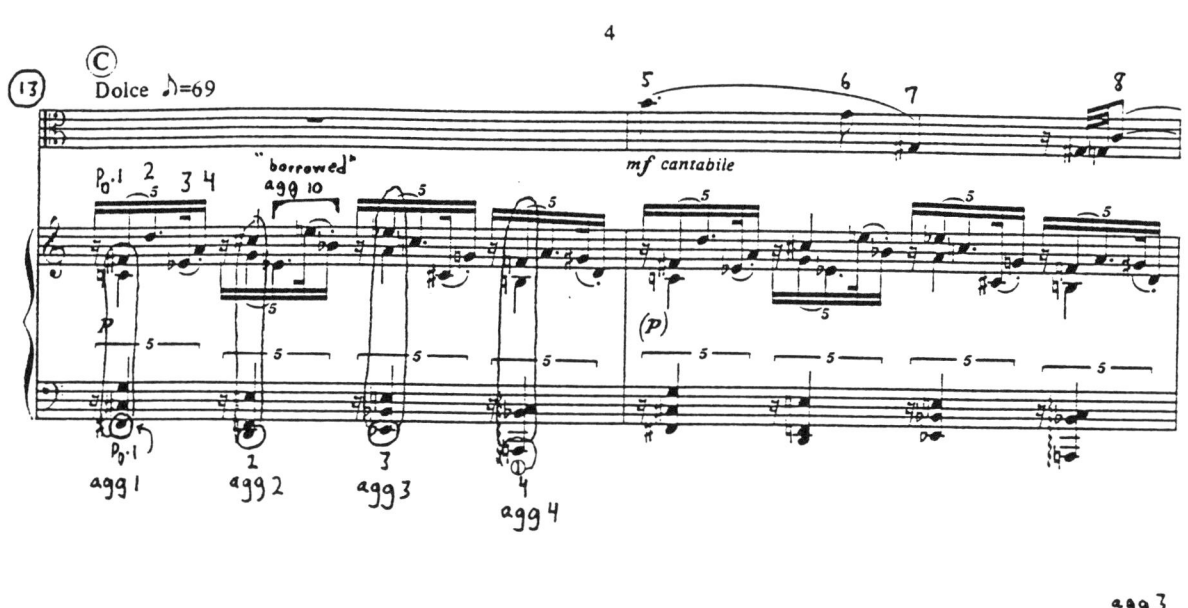

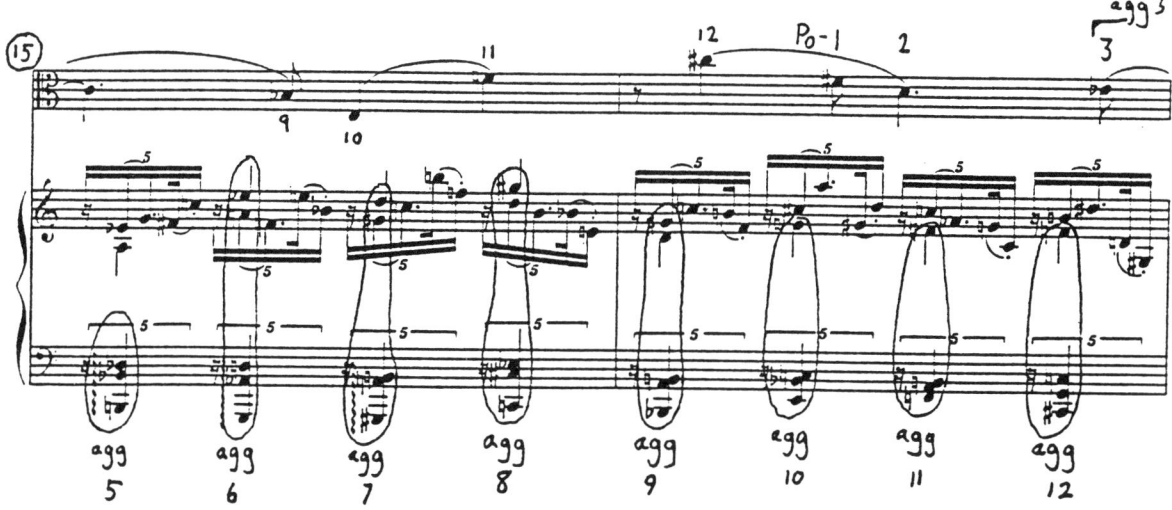

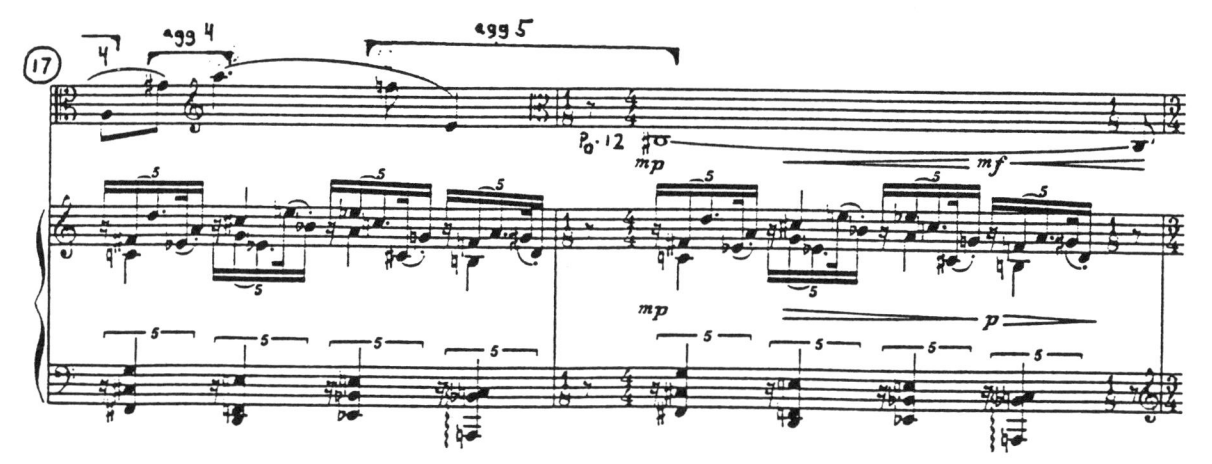

① Roll chord, if necessary, whenever chord is too large for hand.
414-41162

Krosnick Soli
for Solo Cello
6/20/83 – 7/7/83
Maestoso
♪ = 52
★2 = break chords, (as in Bach) bottom to top & back to bottom held notes
★3 suggested as easier by Joel (also on pg 5)
Dolce
MUSIC MASTERS
1

for
soprano, oboe, Piano
Ralph Shapey
Maestoso
Prologue
Praís'd be
soprano
f Prais'--d be
Prais'd be
The fa--thom-
oboe
Ro-12
Sop
--less the
U--mi-verse be
Prais'd
Prais'd
Be
ob

Sonore
♩ = 50
I
Master of the Universe
Sop
ob
Pno
Mas----Ter
of the
u---mi---verse
us our--r
me---ssi--ah
simile
MUSIC MASTERS

(agg 4)
agg 5
agg 6
Sop
we have no more strength To suffer Show me a sign
ob
(agg 5)
agg 6
Pno
simile
agg 10
agg 11
agg 12
(agg 6)
(agg 6)
o God(d) d o God(d) d o-the-wise
agg 7
agg 8
agg 1
agg 2
agg 3

H
(agg 6)
agg 7
3
Sop
o-ther-wise
I re-bel
agg 8
R0-5
re--bel I a-
(agg 8)
agg 4 ("borrowed")
agg 9
ob
R0 9
R0 4
Pno
agg 4
agg 5
agg 6
agg 7
agg 8
agg 9
agg 10
P0-1
P0-2
-gainst thee
Go(d) --do Go(d) - - - - d
R0-12
R0-11
R0 2
P0-11
R0-1
P0-12
MUSIC MASTERS

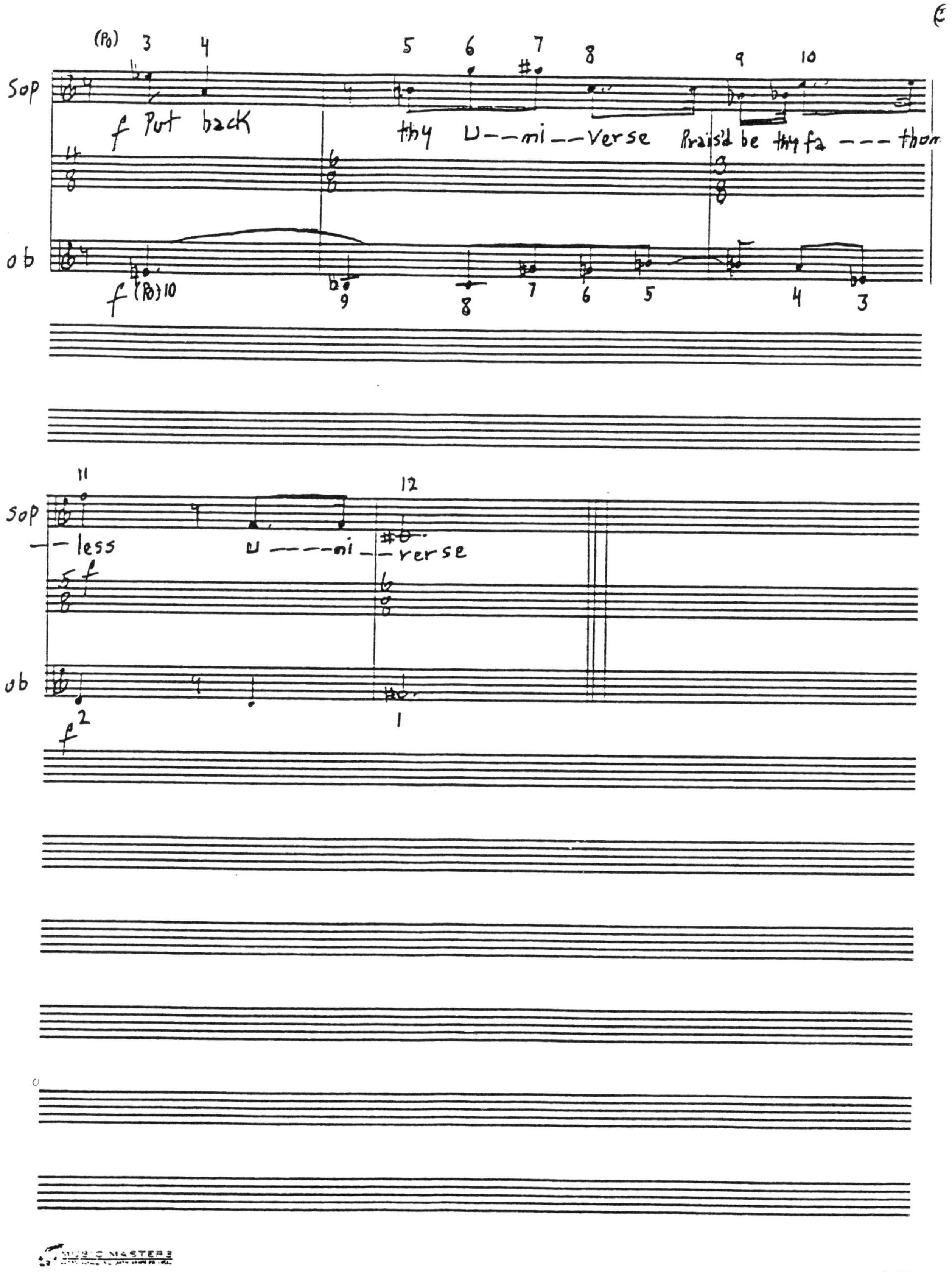
E
Sop
ob
(Po)
f Put back
thy U--mi--verse
Prais'd be thy fa---thom
-less
u----mi--verse

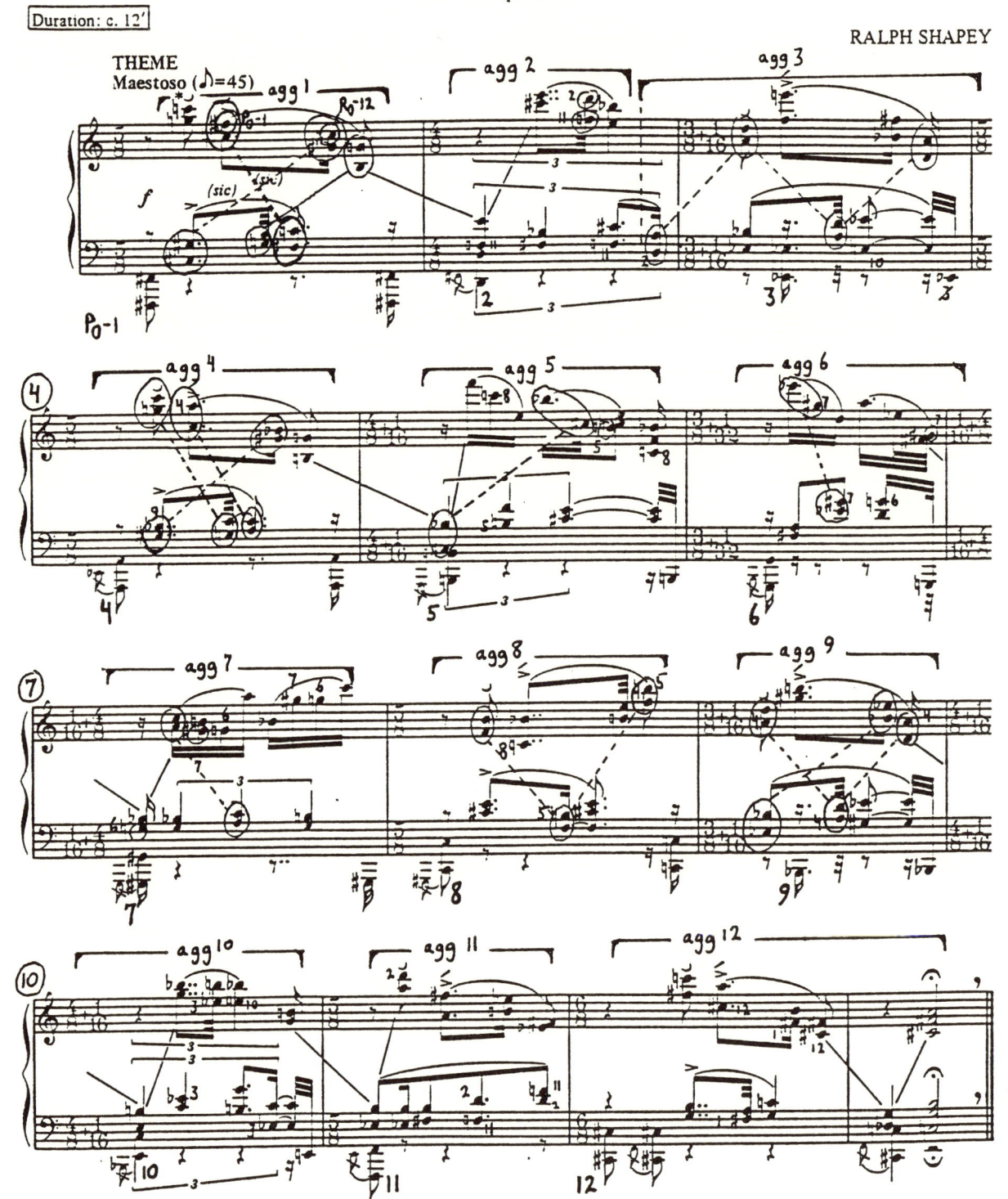

Theme Plus Ten
for Harpsichord

Commissioned by and dedicated to Robert Conant

RALPH SHAPEY

Duration: c. 12'

*The symbol ⌣ indicates an upbeat (weak); the symbol / indicates a downbeat (strong).

VARIATION I

Veloce (♪=♩=90)

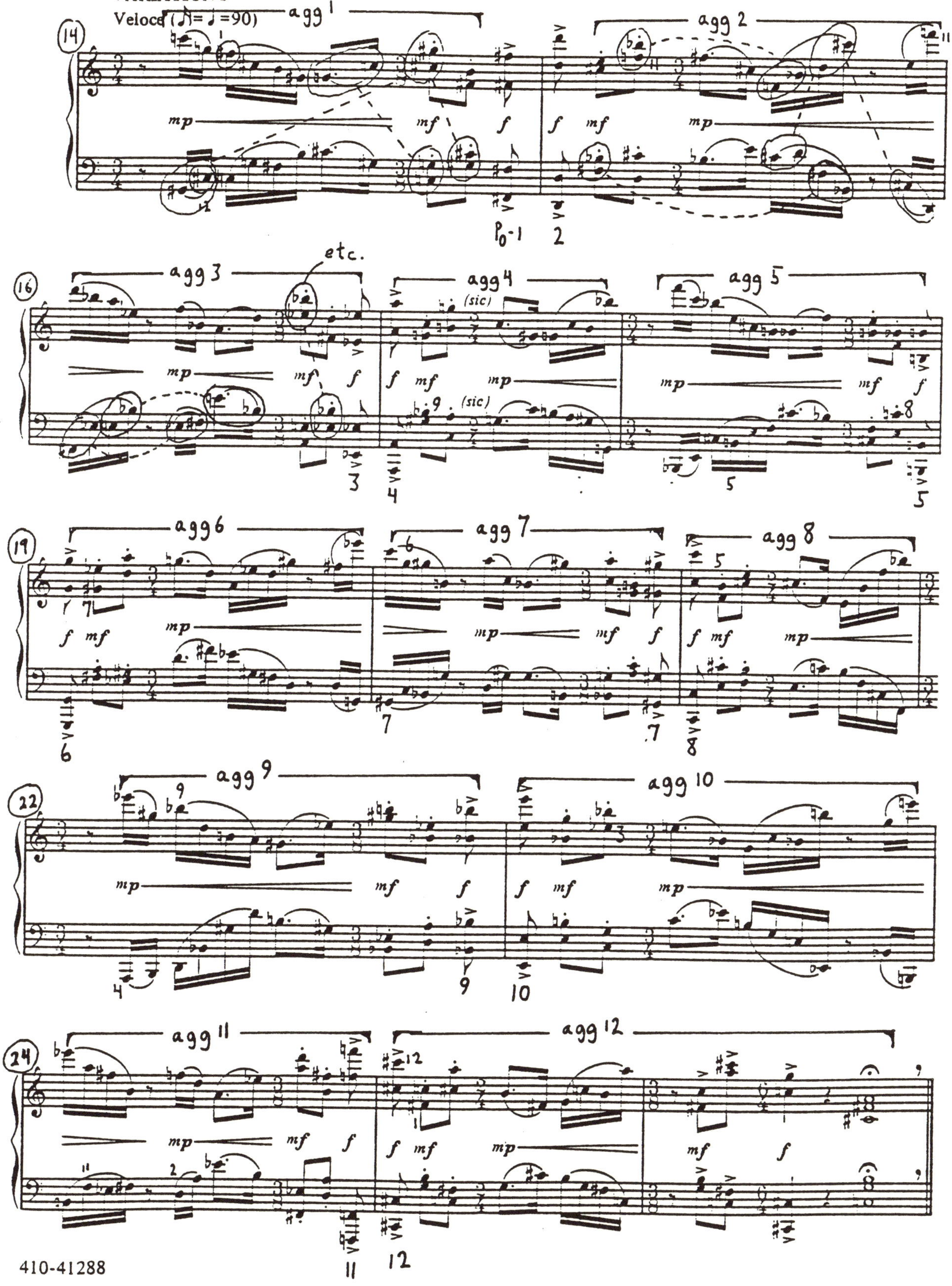

VARIATION II

Vivo (♩. = ♩=60)

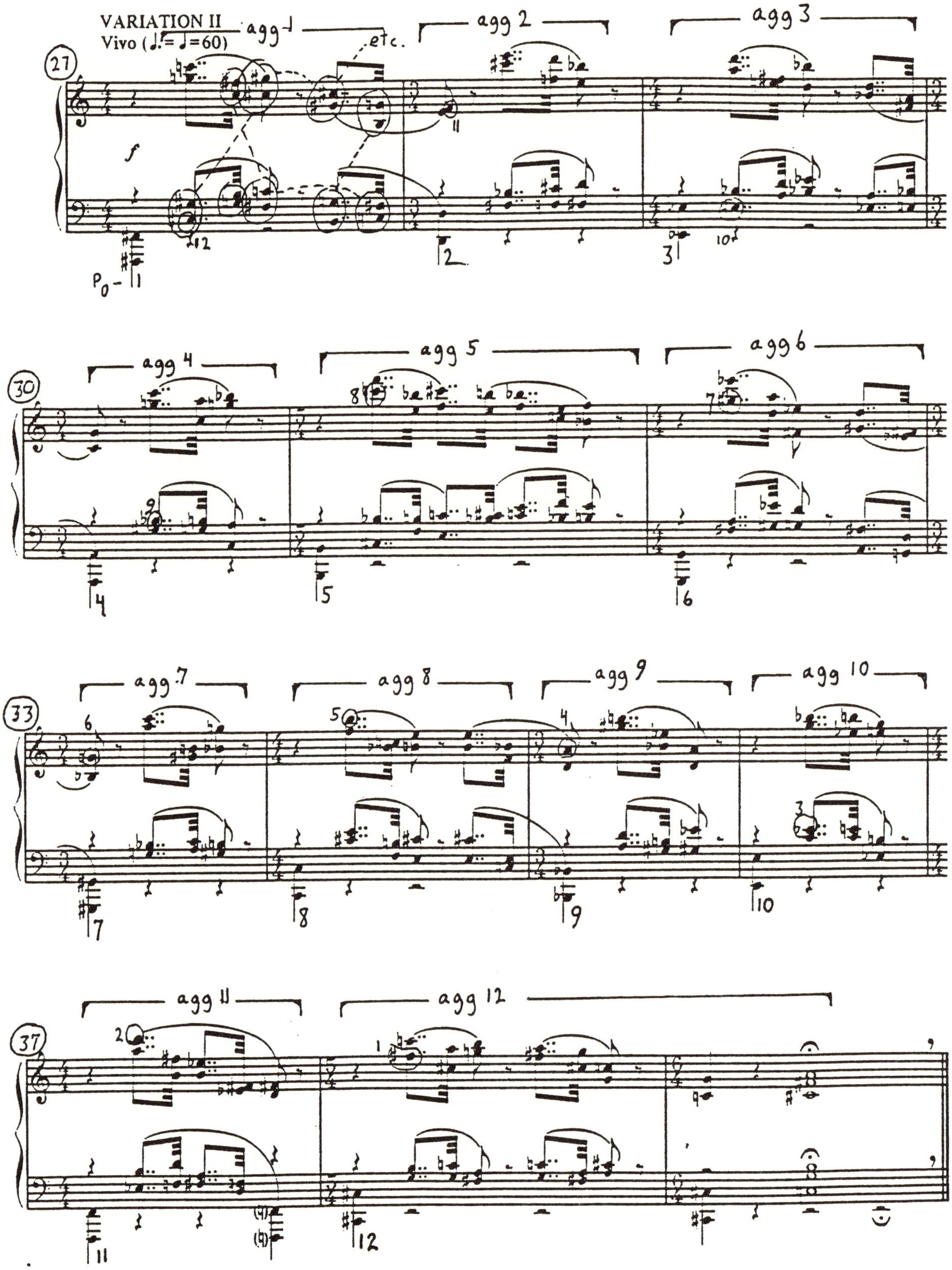

410-41288

CONCERT SCORE

CONCERTANTE NO. II FOR
ALTO SAXOPHONE AND FOURTEEN PLAYERS
I. VARIATIONS

RALPH SHAPEY

Maestoso ♩=42

agg 5
agg 6
agg 7
agg 8
agg 9
agg 10
agg 11
PICC.
OBOE
CLAR
BSN
HORN
P. TPT
B TBN
PER I
PER II
PER II
SAX
VLN
VLA
CELLO
BASS
MUSIC MASTERS

agg 11
agg 12
agg 11
agg 12
A
Brio
PICC
OBOE
CLAR
BSN
Change to Bass Bassoon
HORN
P TPT
B TBN
PER I
PER II
PER III
Roto drums
Timpani
SAX
VLN
VLA
CELLO
BASS
(sic)
A
MUSIC MASTERS

90

10
agg 5
agg 6
agg 5
SAX
(sax)
(sic
TPT
(pizz)
CELLO
Tom
BD
Cym.
Timp.
Roto
PER I
PER III
12
agg 9
agg 10
agg 11
14
agg 12
MUSIC MASTERS

(sax, m.13)
6
15
(pizz.)
Tom
BD
Cym.
Timp.
B
Somoro
Bravura
arco
* alla Bach
(sic)
MUSIC MASTERS

APPENDIX B

Works Arranged by Medium / Instrumental Forces

CHAMBER WORKS

Title	Entry No.	Page No.
Brass Quintet	48	35
Chamber Symphony for 10 Solo Players	45	34
Concertante No. I for trumpet and ten players	96	50
Concerto for Clarinet and Chamber Group	19	26
Concerto Grosso for Woodwind Quintette	80	45
Configurations	51	36
Constellations for Ten Instruments	129	61
Convocation for Chamber Group	43	33
De Profundis for Solo Doublebass and Instruments	38	32
Dinosaur Annex for Violin, Glockenspiel, Vibraphone and Marimba	128	60
Discourse Encore for Violin, Clarinet, Cell and Piano	131	61
Discourse I for Four Instruments	42	33
Discourse II	84	47
Duo for Viola and Piano	25	28
Duo Variations for Violin and Cello	100	52
Evocation No.1 for Violin with Piano and Percussion	32	30
Evocation No. 2 for Cello, Percussion and Piano	73	43
Evocation No. 3 for Viola and Piano	79	45
Evocation No. 4 for Violin, Cello and Piano	121	58
Fanfares for Brass Quintet	78	45
Fantasy	85	47
Five for Violin and Piano	39	32
Four Etudes for Violin	76	44
Gottlieb Duo for Piano and Percussion	89	48
Inventions for Piano and Percussion	122	59
Kroslish Sonate for Cello and Piano	98	51
Lullaby for Soprano and Flute	123	59
Mann Duo for Violin and Viola	86	47
Movement of Varied Movements for Two	119	58
Movements for Woodwind Quintet	36	31
Oboe Quartet for Oboe, Violin, Viola, and Cello	15	24

Partita for Violin and 13 Players	56	37
Partita-Fantasia for Cello and Sixteen Players	58	38
Piano Trio	21	26
Piece for Violin and Instruments	44	33
Poeme	54	37
Quintet for String Quartet and Piano	4	22
Rhapsodie for Cello and Piano	124	59
Rhapsodie for Oboe and Piano	26	28
Soli for Percussion Duo	116	57
Sonata Appassionata for Cello and Piano	130	61
Sonata for Cello and Piano	17	25
Sonata for Oboe and Piano	12	24
Sonata for Violin and Piano	7	22
String Quartet No. 1	2	21
String Quartet No. 2	6	22
String Quartet No. 3	8	23
String Quartet No. 4	16	25
String Quartet No. 6	49	35
String Quartet No. 7	65	40
String Quartet No. 8	125	59
String Quartet No. 9	126	60
String Trio	52	36
Three Concert Pieces for Chamber Orchestra	63	39
Three Concert Pieces for Young Players	60	39
Three for Six	74	43
Trio 1992	120	58
Trio Concertante for Violin, Piano and Percussion	127	60
Trio for Violin, Cello, and Piano	20	26
Variations for Viola and Nine Players	111	55

KEYBOARD WORKS

Title	Entry No.	Page No.
Birthday Piece	46	34
Deux	59	38
Form	33	30
Fromm Variations (31 Variations) for Piano	67	41
Harmaxiemanda for Piano	92	49
Intermezzo for Dulcimer and Keyboards	117	57
Mutations I for Piano	24	27
Mutations II	55	37
Passacaglia for Piano	82	46
Piece in the Form of Sonata-Variations for Piano	18	25
Reyem (or Musical Offering for Flute, Violin, and Piano)	62	39
Seven for Piano Four Hands	47	34
Seven Little Pieces for Piano	9	23
Short Piece for Piano Solo	23	27
Sonance for Carillon	50	35
Sonata No.1 for Piano	3	21
Sonata Profundo	133	62
Sonata Variations for Piano	28	29
Suite of Four Pieces for Piano	13	24
Tango Variations on a Tango Cantus for Piano	95	50
Theme Plus Ten for Harpsichord	107	54
Three Essays on Thomas Wolf for Piano	5	22
Twenty-one Variations for Piano	71	42
Variations for Organ	97	51
Variations On A Cantus for Piano	110	55

VOCAL WORKS

Title	Entry No.	Page No.
Cantata	10	23
Centennial Celebration for Soprano, Mezzo Soprano, Tenor, Bass, and Twelve Players	118	57
Dimensions for Soprano and 23 Instruments	40	32
Goethe Songs for Soprano and Piano	132	61
In Memoriam for Soprano, Baritone and Nine Players	106	53
Incantations for Soprano and Ten Instruments	41	33
O Jerusalem for Soprano and Flute	68	41
Praise (Oratorio for Bass-Baritone, Double Chorus, and Chamber Group)	64	40
Psalm II	93	50
Soliloquy for Narrator, String Quartet, and Percussion	34	30
Songs (for Soprano and Piano)	81	46
Songs No. 2 for Soprano and Four Instruments	94	50
Songs of Ecstasy for Soprano with Piano, Percussion, and Tape	61	39
Songs of Joy for Soprano and Piano	109	54
Songs of Life	112	55
Songs of Love (And My Beloved is Mine)	105	53
Songs of Love (I am My Beloved's)	104	53
String Quartet No. 5 with Female Voice	27	28
Thanks to the Human Heart for Soprano Voices and Piano	113	56
The Covenant for Soprano and 16 Players and Prerecorded Tapes	70	42
This Day for Female Voice and Piano	37	31
Trilogy (Song of Songs) I	72	43
Trilogy (Song of Songs) II	75	44
Trilogy (Song of Songs) III	77	44
Walking Upright	29	29
Psalm I for Soprano, Oboe, and Piano	90	49

ORCHESTRAL WORKS

Title	Entry No.	Page No.
Challenge—The Family of Man	22	27
Concertante No. II	108	54
Concerto Fantastique for Symphony Orchestra	115	56
Concerto for Cello, Piano, and String Orchestra	103	52
Double Concerto for Violin, Cello, and Orchestra	83	47
Fantasy for Symphony Orchestra	11	23
Groton Three Movements for Young Orchestra	91	49
Inspiration	1	21
Invocation—Concerto for Violin and Orchestra	31	29
Ontogeny for Symphony Orchestra	30	29
Passacaglia for Piano and Orchestra	88	48
Rituals for Symphony Orchestra	35	31
Songs of Eros for Soprano, Symphony Orchestra, and Tape	69	42
Symphonie Concertante	99	51
Symphony No.1	14	24

SOLO WORKS (OTHER THAN KEYBOARD)

Title	Entry No.	Page No.
For Solo Trumpet	57	38
Krosnick Soli for Solo Cello	87	48
Mann Soli for Solo Violin	101	52
Partita for Solo Violin	53	36
Soli for Solo Percussion	102	52
Sonate No.1 for Solo Violin	66	41
Two for One for Solo Snare Drum	114	56

APPENDIX C

Discography

PREFACE TO THE DISCOGRAPHY

There are twenty recordings of works by Ralph Shapey. These occur on four labels. The discography is organized by record manufacturer, and within each of these sections in the numerical order of the serial number for ease of reference. The catalogue entry number of the recorded work is cited next, followed by the title and performers. The technical information about the recordings provided on the record jacket varies. An at tempt has been made to make the entries as consistent as possible. Works by other com posers on each recording are listed but without detailed information. An index of recorded works by catalogue entry number keyed to recording serial numbers is provided at the end of the discography.

DISCOGRAPHY

FRIENDS OF FOUR HAND MUSIC

(no serial no.) (entry no. 47) - *Seven For Piano, Four Hands* (1963). Milton and Peggy Salkind, pn. Liner notes by Andrew Imbrie. Commissioned, recorded, and produced by The Friends of Four Hand Music, 1645 Edith St., Berkely, Calif. (no recording date cited).

CRI RECORDS

CRI SD 141 (entry no. 32) - *Evocation No. 1* for violin, with piano and percussion (1959). Matthew Raimondi, vln.; Yehudi Wyner, pn.; Paul Price, percussion. (Also featured on the recording: Yehudi Wyner: *Serenade For Seven Instruments*).

CRI SD 232 (entry no. 41) - *Incantations* for soprano and ten instruments (1961). Bethany Beardsley, sop.; The Contemporary Chamber Players of the University of Chicago; Ralph Shapey, cond.. (Also featured on the recording: John MacIver Perkins: *Music for Thirteen Players* (1964), and Caprice (1963). Both works recorded by Walter Key (no date given). Liner notes by Carter Harman.

CRI SD 275 (entry no. 35 and 49) - *Rituals* for symphony orchestra (1959). London Sinfonietta with Ray Swingfield, a. sax.; Richard Fudoli, t. sax.; Roy Willoc, bar. sax.; W. Thomas McKinley, pn.; Ralph Shapey, cond. Recorded by Eric Tomlinson (no date given). (Entry no. 49) - *String Quartet No. 6* (1963). The Lexington Quartet of the Contemporary Chamber Players of the University of Chicago: Elliot Golub, vln.; Everett Zlatoff-Mirsky, vln.; Roger Moulton, vla.; John Hill, vcl.. Recorded by Bruce Swedien (Also featured on the recording: Seymour Schifrin: *Three Pieces for Orchestra*).

CRI SD 355 (entry no. 64) - *Praise* An oratorio for bass-baritone, chorus, and chamber orchestra (1971). Paul Geiger, bass-bar.; The Contemporary Chamber Players of the University of Chicago; Ralph Shapey, cond. Recording released 1976.

CRI SD 391 (entry no. 65) - *String Quartet No. 7* (1972). Quartet of the Contemporary Chamber Players of the University of Chicago: Elliot Golub, vln.; Everett Zlatoff-Mirsky, vln.; Lee Lane, vla.; Barbara Haffner, vcl.. Recorded in Chicago by Richard Mintel, April, 1977.

CRI SD 423 (entry no. 26) - *Rhapsodie* for oboe and piano (1957). James Ostryniec, ob.; Charles Wourinen, pn.. (Also featured on the recording: George Rochberg: *La Bocca Della Verita* for oboe and piano; Ruth Crawford Seeger: *Diaphonic Suite No. 1* for solo oboe; Gunther Schuller: *Trio* for oboe, viola, and horn; Joseph Julian: *Wave Canon* for oboe and tape; Lawrence Singer: *Work* for solo oboe). All works recorded by David Hancock, April - July 1979, New York City.

CRI SD 428 (entry no. 67) - *Fromm Variations* for Piano (1973). Robert Black, pn.. Recorded by David Hancock, New York, February, 1980.

CRI SD 435 (entry no. 70) - *The Covenant* for soprano, sixteen players and two pre-recorded tapes (1977). Elsa Charlston, sop.; The Contemporary Chamber Players of the University of Chicago; Ralph Shapey, cond.; voice tapes recorded by Elsa Charlston and Gershon Silins, bar.. Recorded by Richard Mintel, Chicago, September, 1981.

CRI SD 496 (entry no. 71) - *Twenty-One Variations for Piano* (1978). Wanda Maximilien, pn.. (Also featured on the recording: Gerald Chenoweth: *Three Musics for Piano Solo,* Robert Moevs: *Una Collana Musicale* (1977): Nos. 1, 3, 4, 7, 8, 9, 13). All works recorded by David Hancock, New York City, spring, 1983.

CRI SD 501 (entry no. 3) - *Sonata* for piano (1952). Wanda Maximilien, pn.. Recorded by Roger Rhodes, New York City, January, 1984. (Also featured on the recording: Ruth Crawford Seeger: *Three Songs* for alto, oboe, piano, and percussion; Witold Lutoslawski: *Epitaph* for piano; Charles Ives: *Adagio Sostenuto* for string quartet and piano; Otto Leuning: *Legend* for oboe and strings).

CRI SD 509 (entry no. 74) - *Three for Six* (1979). New York New Music Ensemble: Jayne Rosenfield, fl.; Laura Flax, cl.; Daniel Druckman, pc; Alan Feinberg, pn.; Cyrus Stevens, vln.; Eric Bartlett, vcl.; Robert Black, cond.. Recorded by David Hancock (no date given). (Also featured on the recording: Shulamit Ran: *Apprehensions*).

NEW WORLD RECORDS

NW 254 (entry no. 51) - *Configurations* for flute and piano (1964). Sophie Sollberger, fl.; Robert Black, pn.. (Also featured on the recording: Harvey Sollberger: *Sunflowers;* Robert Morris: *Motet on Doo-Dah;* Robert Hall Lewis: *Inflections I;* Andrew Imbrie: *Three Sketches;* Robert Erickson: *General Speech*). All works recorded at Columbia Recording Studios, 30th Street, New York.

NW 333 (entry no. 85) - *Fantasy* for violin and piano (1983). Maryvonne Le Dizes-Richard, vln.; Jean-Claude Henriot, pn.. (Also featured on the recording: Elliott Carter: *Riconoscenza,* Tod Machover: *Hidden Sparks;* John Melby: *Concerto for Violin and Computer–Synthesized Tape*). All works recorded at IRCAM (Institut de Recherche et Coordination Accoustique /

DISCOGRAPHY

Musique), Centre Georges Pompidou, Paris, January, 1985. Liner notes by Tim Page.

NW 355-2 (CD) (entry no. 96 and 98) - *Concertante No. 1* for Trumpet and Ten Players (1984). Ronald Anderson, tpt.; The Contemporary Chamber Players of the University of Chicago: Carole Morgan, fl. / a. fl. / picc.; Marc Fink, ob. / E. hn.; John Bruce Yeh, cl. / E flat cl. / b. cl.; Peter Brusen, bass.; Collins Trier, bsn.; Douglas Hill, hn.; Peter Labella, vln.; Sharon Polifrone, vla.; Elaine Scott Banks, vcl.; Douglas Waddell, pc; Ralph Shapey, cond. Recorded at Mandel Hall, Chicago, April 1987. (Entry no. 98) - *Kroslish Sonate* for cello and piano (1985). Joel Krosnick, vcl.; Gilbert Kalish, pn. Recorded at the Sommer Center, Concordia College, Bronxville, New York, April, 1987. (Also featured on the recording: Faye-Ellen Silverman: *Restless Winds, Speaking Alone,* and *Passing Fancies*).

NW 377-2 (CD) (entry no. 48) - *Brass Quintet* (1963). The American Brass Quintet: Raymond Mase and Chris Gekker, tpt.; David Wakefield, hn.; Michael Powell, t. tmb.; Robert Biddlecome, b. tmb. (Also featured on the recording: Maurice Wright: *Quintet*; William Bolcom: *Quintet*; Jacob Druckman: *Other Voices* for Brass Quintet). All works recorded at RCA Studio A, New York, October 10 - 12, 1988. Liner notes by Elaine Guregian.

OPUS ONE RECORDINGS

Opus One 106 (entry no. 81) - Songs for Soprano (1982). Elsa Charlston, sop.; Lambert Orkin, pn. (Also featured on the recording: Frank Martin: *Quatre Sonnets (A Cassandre)*). Both works recorded in New York, 1984. Liner notes submitted by the artists and compiled by Max Schubel.

Opus One 121 (entry no. 68) - *O Jerusalem* for soprano and flute (1974). Elsa Charlston, sop.; Carole Morgan, fl. (also featured on the recording: Glenn Gass: *Breathless,* Frank Stemper: Chamelion, and *Two Pieces for Baby.* Liner notes by the artists, compiled by Max Schubel (no recording locations or dates cited).

RECORDED WORKS IN ORDER OF ENTRY NO.

ENTRY NO.	RECORDING
47	Friends of Four Hand Music.
	CRI
3	CRI
	CRI SD 501
26	CRI SD 423
32	CRI SD 141
35	CRI SD 275
41	CRI SD 232
49	CRI SD 275
64	CRI SD 355
65	CRI SD 391
67	CRI SD 428
70	CRI SD 435
71	CRI SD 496
74	CRI SD 509
	NEW WORLD
48	NW 377-2 (CD)
51	NW 254
85	NW 333
96	NW 355-2 (CD)
98	NW 355-2 (CD)

OPUS ONE

68	Opus One 121
81	Opus One 106

BIBLIOGRAPHY

LIST OF AUTHORED ARTICLES CITED

Anderson, Jess. "Controlling Interest," *Isthmus,* Friday, May 10, 1996 (entry no. 126).

Anderson, Ronald. "US-Trompeter im Alleingang," *Mónchener Merkur,* Thursday, November 13, 1969 (entry no. 57).

Baker, Edward. "Interesting Concert Ends N.D.M. Season," *The Seattle Times,* Friday, March 22, 1968 (entry no. 41).

Belt, Byron. "Choral Recordings For Holiday gifts," *Long Island Press,* Sunday, November 28, 1976 (entry no. 64).

Buell, Richard. "Nancy Cirillo Tells No Lies," *The Boston Globe,* Wednesday, January 28, 1981 (entry no. 32).

_____. "New Pieces of Music That Deserve to Live," *The Boston Globe,* Tuesday, February 20, 1990 (entry no. 74).

Burwasser, Peter. "Shapey's Music: The Orchestra Premieres a New Work By America's Most Underrated Composer," *City Paper* (Philadelphia), Friday, April 3–Friday, April 10, 1987 (entry no. 99).

Caruso, Michael. "Shapey Constitutional Work Disappointing," *Chestnut Hill Local* (Philadelphia), Thursday, April 9, 1987 (entry no. 99).

Cera, Stephen. "N.Y. New Music Ensemble Offers World Premieres," *The Sun Today* (Baltimore), Monday, January 26, 1981 (entry no. 74).

Cook, David. "Violinist Plays Display Pieces," *Tallahassee, Fla. Democrat,* Sunday, March 5, 1972 (entry no. 49).

Cooper, Paul. "Once Festival Concerts," *The Ann Arbor News,* Monday, February 19, 1962 (entry no. 36)

Crawford, Richard. "'Once' Festival: Dorian Quintet Excels," *The Michigan Daily,* Sunday, February 18, 1962 (entry no. 36).

Croan, Robert. "New Music Ensemble City's Most Significant," *Pittsburgh Post-Gazette,* Tuesday, March 7, 1978 (entry no. 68).

Crutchfield, Will. "Music: The Philadelphia," *The New York Times,* Thursday, April 9, 1987 (entry no. 99).

Davis, Peter G. "Meet the Virtuosos of New Music," *The New York Times,* Sunday, April 27, 1975 (entry no. 32).

_____. "Music," *New York,* February 6, 1984 (entry no. 83).

Delacoma, Wayne. "Premieres Highlight High Night of Music," *Chicago Sun Times,* Sunday, April 26, 1987 (entry no. 96).

_____. "CSO Hosts Birthday Bash for Maverick Composer," *Chicago Sun Times,* Thursday, November 7, 1991 (entry no. 115).

_____. "CSO's Dazzling, Difficult in 'Concerto Fantastique,'" *Chicago Sun Times,* Friday, November 22, 1991 (entry no. 115).

_____. "New Music Groups Put Different Spin on Classics With Festival Concerts," *Chicago Sun Times,* April 16, 1989 (entry no. 108).

_____. "Ralph Shapey, In Seven Short Movements," *Chicago Sun Times,* Sunday, November 17, 1991 (entry no. 115).

Devoe, David E. (No title: review of CRI disc *31 Variations for Piano*), *Fort Wayne News - Sentinel,* Saturday, May 9, 1981 (entry no. 70).

Doerr, Alan. "Lebow Excels in Recital of Taxing Piano Works," *The Washington Post,* Monday, May 3, 1965 (entry no. 46).

Dyer, Richard. "One Evening, Two String Quartets," *The Boston Globe,* Wednesday, August 16, 1995 (entry no. 125).

Erickson, Raymond. "Concert: Juilliard Presents Ralph Shapey's 'Covenant,'" *The New York Times,* Sunday, May 20, 1979 (entry no. 70).

_____. "Husband - Wife Duo of Pianists Gives First Recital Here," *The New York Times,* Thursday, April 29, 1971 (entry no. 59).

Etheridge, Tom. "CSO Honors Shapey in Birthday Celebration," *The Chicago Tribune,* Tuesday, November 19, 1991 (entry no. 115).

Frankenstein, Alfred. "Mills Festival Experiment," *The San Francisco Chronicle,* Tuesday, May 28, 1963 (entry no. 20).

Fried, Alexander. "Odd Musical Sounds At Mills: Experiments in Tone," *San Francisco Examiner,* Tuesday, May 28, 1963 (entry no. 20).

Gowen, Bill. "Shapey Returns To CSO with 'Fantastique,'" *The Chicago Daily Herald,* Thursday, November 21, 1991 (entry no. 115).

Haaden, Nikki. "Record Reviews," *The Chattanooga Times,* Saturday, June 12, 1982 (entry no. 67).

Harmon, Donald. "Shapey: Incantations. Perkins: Music for Thirteen Players," *High Fidelity Magazine,* June, 1969 (entry no. 41).

Helm, Everett. "New Sounds for the Avant Garde," *San Francisco Sunday Chronicle,* June 17, 1962 (entry no. 40).

Henahan, Donal. "Current Chronical." *Musical Quarterly,* vol. 53, no. 2 (1967). (entry nos. 30 and 31).

_____. "Music: Moderns Festival," *The New York Times,* Thursday, January 26, 1984 (entry no. 83).

_____. "Incantations: Poetry With Notes," *Chicago Daily News,* Wednesday, February 19, 1968 (entry no. 41).

_____. "Remarkable Mandel Hall Concert: New Music By Four Good Men," *Chicago Daily News,* Friday, May 27, 1966 (entry no. 30).

Henken, John. "Shapey: Praise," *Los Angeles Times,* Sunday, October 22, 1978 (entry no. 64).

Holland, Bernard. "Music: Debuts in Review: Rich Week of Recitals Highlighted by Avo Kouyoumdjian, Prize-Winning Pianist," *The New York Times,* Sunday, October 24, 1982 (entry no. 79).

_____. "Music: Shapey," *The New York Times,* Wednesday, April 20, 1983 (entry no. 82).

Hoover, Joanne Sheehy. "Song of Songs, No. 1," *The Washington Post,* Saturday, March 1, 1980 (entry no. 72).

Hughes, Allen. "Music: Schuller Leads Four New Works," *The New York Times,* Friday, April 6, 1979 (entry no. 58).

Hume, Paul. "New Shapey Trio High On Calendar," *The Washington Post,* Wednesday, January 5, 1966 (entry no. 52).

_____. "New Works Are Skillfully Performed By Iowa Quartet in Kindler Concert," *The Washington Post,* Tuesday, January 11, 1966 (entry no. 52).

_____. "Solo Pianists Return as Duo," *The Washington Post,* Tuesday, April 15, 1969 (entry no. 59).

Jacobson, Bernard. "A Spate of Musical Premieres," *Chicago Daily News,* Monday, May 27, 1968 (entry no. 31).

_____. "'Songs of Ecstasy' Highlight concert," *Chicago Daily News,* Monday, May 26, 1969 (entry no. 61).

_____. "Shapey's Partita Tops Evening," *Chicago Daily News,* Thursday January 26, 1967 (entry no. 56).

Joseph McLellan. "Coloristic Resources," *The Washington Post,* Monday, May 17, 1976 (entry no. 55).

Kerner, Leighton. "Kerner's Consumer Guide," *The Village Voice,* January 21–27, 1981 (entry no. 67).

_____. "Psalm and Fury," *The Village Voice,* Tuesday, August 22, 1989 (entry no. 103).

Kosman, Joshua. "Septet Gives Punch to New Music Program," *San Francisco Chronicle,* Wednesday, February 12, 1992 (entry no. 74).

_____. "Thoroughly Modern Trio Music," *San Francisco Chronicle,* Wednesday, February 12, 1992 (entry no. 127).

Kozinn, Allan. "A String Quartet of True Fraternity," *The New York Times,* Monday, February 6, 1989 (entry no. 42). Thursday, October 27, 1994 (entry no. 125).

_____. "Quirky Harmony From Maracas and Synthesizer," *The New York Times,* Wednesday, May 11, 1994 (entry no. 129).

_____. "Recent Chamber Works," *The New York Times,* Monday, February 6, 1989 (entry no. 42).

_____. "Surveying The Twentieth Century," *The New York Times,* Wednesday, April 26, 1996 (entry no. 121).

Lang, Paul Henry. "Music: The Fromm Foundation," *The New York Herald Tribune,* Sunday, May 14, 1962 (entry no. 40).

Marsh, Robert C. "Bavarian Warmth and a Study In Contrast," *Chicago Sun Times,* Monday, April 21, 1978 (entry no. 70).

_____. "Cold Winds of Apathy Chill CCP," *Chicago Sun Times,* Tuesday, March 11, 1980 (entry no. 72).

_____. "Finer Arts," *Chicago Sun Times,* Friday, November 22, 1991 (entry no. 115).

McCorkle, Donald. "Iowa Quartet Superb in Kindler Concert," *The Evening Star* (Washington, D. C.), Tuesday, January 11, 1966 (entry no. 52).

Mercel, Constance. "Howard Lebow Exhibits New Directions in Music," *Vassar Miscellany News* (Poughkeepsie, NY), Wednesday, November 8, 1961 (entry no. 33).

Myers, Theodore. "Classical Gems," *Newsweek,* March 7, 1977 (entry no. 64).

Noren, Ann. "Why This Oratorio," *Chicago Sun Times,* Sunday, February 22, 1976 (entry no. 64).

Novik, Ylda. "Lorenz and Bronstein Top Flight In Pianistics," *The Evening Star* (Washington, D.C.), Tuesday, April 15, 1969 (entry no. 59).

Page, Tim. "Modern Sounds On the Organ," *The New York Times,* Sunday, March 2, 1986 (entry no. 97).

_____. "Tanglewood's Contemporary Bag," *Newsday,* Monday, August 7, 1989 (entry no. 103).

Patner, Andrew. "Modern Works Work Well," *The Chicago Sun Times,* Monday, April 25, 1994 (entry no. 123).

_____. "Shapey Continues to Enlighten," *Chicago Sun Times,* Tuesday, April 4, 1995 (entry nos. 112 and 128).

_____. "Last Fromm Concert Starts 'Conversations,'" *The Chicago Sun Times,* Tuesday, April 16, 1996 (entry no. 41).

Perkins, Francis D. "Music: Quartet Pays Tribute in Concert," *The New York Times,* Thursday, May 27, 1954 (entry no. 16).

Pettitt, Stephen. "A Sample of Themes," *The New York Times,* Wednesday, June 11, 1988 (entry no. 68).

Pincus, Andrew. "Tanglewood Festival Concert Yields Promising New Work," *The Berkshire Eagle,* Wednesday, August 16, 1995 (entry no. 125).

_____. "Shapey and Firsova Pieces Exhibit Contrasting Power," *The Berkshire Eagle,* Friday, August 4, 1989 (entry no. 103).

Potter, Kieth. "Records and Recordings: Rituals," Gramophone, September, 1976 (entry no. 35).

Putnam, Thomas. "Shapey Music Played at UB," *Buffalo Courier - Express,* Wednesday, June 11, 1980 (entry no. 51).

Reich, Howard. "Variations' Victorious—World Premiere of Shapey's Composition is Compelling Fare," *Chicago Tribune,* Monday, April 23, 1990 (entry no. 111).

Rich, Allan. "Festival Contemporarily Exemplary," *Los Angeles Herald Examiner,* Thursday, August 3, 1989 (entry no. 103).

Rockwell, John. Cello: Krosnick And Five Premieres," *The New York Times,* Thursday, April 16, 1981 (entry no. 73).

_____. "Concert: Composers Orchestra," *The New York Times,* Wednesday, May 22, 1981 (entry no. 35).

_____. "Concert: New Music for the Organ," *The New York Times,* Wednesday, March 12, 1986 (entry no. 97).

_____. "Concert: Tanglewood Goes Contemporary," *The New York Times,* Monday, August 3, 1981 (entry no. 36).

_____. "Concert: Tanglewood Goes Contemporary," *The New York Times,* Monday, August 3, 1981 (entry no. 36).

_____. "Music: Mann and Son," *The New York Times,* Friday, January 13, 1984 (entry no. 86).

_____. "Recital: Pair of New Compositions From Chicago," *The New York Times,* Saturday, January 31, 1981 (entry no. 67).

Ross, Alex. "A Master of the Memorably Atonal," *The New York Times,* Tuesday, May 7, 1996 (entry nos. 87 and 121).

Rothstein, Edward. "Music: Alard Strings," *The New York Times,* Thursday, November 3, 1983 (entry no. 2).

Shen, Ted. "Confidence, Skill Mark Composer's Diverse Program," *The Chicago Tribune,* Tuesday, April 4, 1995 (entry no. 112 and 129).

Singer, Samuel. "Group Closes Season With Shapey Concert," *The Philadelphia Inquirer,* Sunday, May 27, 1962 (entry no. 27).

Smoley, Allen. "Shapey: String Quartet No. 7," *American Record Guide,* December, 1978 (entry no. 65).

Sterritt, David. "Winners on Discs: Music in Time and Space," *The Christian Science Monitor,* Monday, May 12, 1969 (entry no. 41).

Strongin, Theodore. "Aeolian Players Offer New Works," *The New York Times,* Thursday, January 25, 1962 (entry no. 42).

_____. "Composer's Showcase Begins Season With a Varied Concert," *The New York Times,* Tuesday, November 29, 1966 (entry no. 49).

_____. "Music: Symphonists Accept Modernists," *Chicago Daily News,* Thursday, January 26, 1967 (entry no. 56).

Thomas, Martha. "New Work Draws On 'Old Masters,'" *South Star* (Philadelphia), Thursday, April 9, 1987 (entry no. 99).

Tommasini, Anthony. "Vibrant, Unsettling Concerto Premieres," *The Boston Globe,* Wednesday, August 2, 1989 (entry no. 103).

Turok, Paul. "New And Noteworthy: A Survey of Interesting New Recordings," *Ovation,* May, 1987 (entry no. 85).

Vinton, John. "Medium Hurts Lebow Recital," *The Evening Star* (Washington, D.C.), Monday, May 3, 1965 (entry no. 46).

Von Rhein, John. "A Night of Schoenberg and Stylistic Derivations," *Chicago Tribune,* Tuesday, March 11, 1980 (entry no. 72).

_____. "Arditti Conquers in Debut Concert," *Chicago Tribune,* Tuesday, March 8, 1988 (entry no. 52).

_____. "CCP Concert Becomes Fine Shapey Affair," *Chicago Tribune,* Sunday, April 26, 1987 (entry no. 96).

_____. "Complete Version of 'Trilogy' Brings Shapey's Vision Into Focus," *Chicago Tribune,* Monday, April 27, 1981 (entry no. 75).

_____. "Ensemble Stays With Tradition As It Turns 25," *Chicago Tribune,* Sunday, April 23, 1989 (entry no. 108).

_____. "Fromm Concert Series Plays Its Finale," *Chicago Tribune,* Tuesday, April 16, 1996 (entry no. 41).

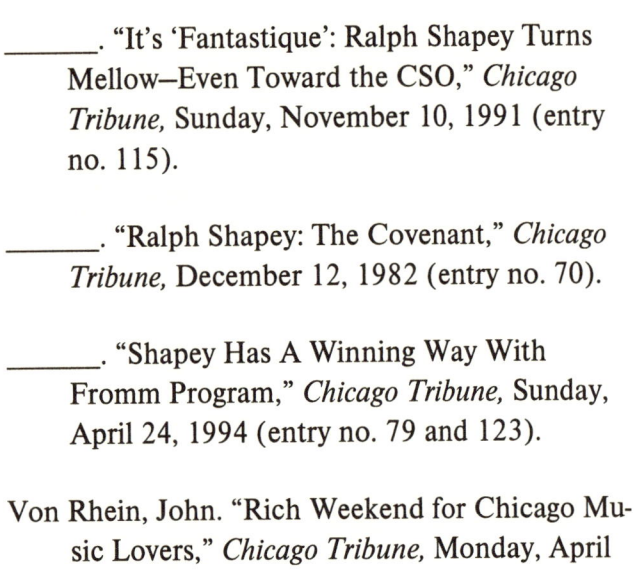

_____. "It's 'Fantastique': Ralph Shapey Turns Mellow—Even Toward the CSO," *Chicago Tribune,* Sunday, November 10, 1991 (entry no. 115).

_____. "Ralph Shapey: The Covenant," *Chicago Tribune,* December 12, 1982 (entry no. 70).

_____. "Shapey Has A Winning Way With Fromm Program," *Chicago Tribune,* Sunday, April 24, 1994 (entry no. 79 and 123).

Von Rhein, John. "Rich Weekend for Chicago Music Lovers," *Chicago Tribune,* Monday, April 17, 1976 (entry no. 55).

_____. "Shapey Directs A Challenging World Premiere," *Chicago Tribune,* Friday, November 22, 1991 (entry no. 115).

_____. "Shapey Ends Shining Career On An Inspirational Note," *Chicago Tribune,* Monday, April 26, 1993 (entry no. 122).

_____. "Shapey Is Saluted As Iconoclast Meets Chicago Institution," *Chicago Tribune,* Tuesday, November 12, 1991 (entry no. 115).

_____. "Shapey Works Highlight Goodman Series," *Chicago Tribune,* Wednesday, April 6, 1983 (entry no. 81).

Webster, Daniel. "Orchestra Plays Constitution Work," *The Philadelphia Enquirer,* Friday, April 3, 1987 (entry no. 99).

Willis, Thomas. "Music of the Baroque Ensemble Sets the Tone With Accent on Happy," *Chicago Tribune,* Monday, April 25, 1977 (entry no. 65).

Willis, Thomas. "Symphony Soars in Campus Concert Despite Confusion," *Chicago Tribune,* Friday, May 27, 1966 (entry no. 30).

LIST OF ANONYMOUS ARTICLES CITED

"Arthur Berger Plays Own Work," *New York Herald Tribune,* Monday, April 7, 1958 (entry no. 24).

"Concert at the 'Y': But is it Music?," *The New York Times,* Thursday, March 24, 1966 (entry no. 51).

"'Dimensions' Adds Humor," *Seattle Post - Intelligencer,* Saturday, May 23, 1968 (entry no. 41).

"Concert features Two U.S. Composers, *The New York Times,* Monday, April 7, 1958 (entry no. 24).

"Composer's Concert," *New York Herald Tribune,* Tuesday, March 28, 1950 (entry no. 6).

"Director Cancels CSO Appearances," *Chicago Tribune,* Tuesday, November 19, 1991 (entry no. 115).

"'Fantastique' Premiere Will Mark University, CSO Centennials," *University of Chicago Chronical,* Thursday, November 7, 1991 (entry no. 115).

"Pittsburgh: Shapey Premiere," *High Fidelity / Musical America,* July, 1978 (entry no. 70).

"Ralph Shapey: Praise," *Nevada State Journal,* Sunday, August 22, 1976 (entry no. 64).

"Record Reviews," *St. Louis Globe Democrat,* Saturday - Sunday, December 20–21, 1980 (entry no. 67).

"Rehearsing World Premiere," *Chicago Daily News,* Saturday-Sunday, February 28–29, 1976 (entry no. 64).

"Schafer Composition Has Great Impact," *Chicago Tribune,* Sunday, May 25, 1969 (entry no. 61).

"Shapey and Others," *The Village Voice,* May 24, 1962 (entry no. 40).

"Two Groups Heard in Chamber Music," *The New York Times,* Tuesday, March 28, 1950. (entry no. 6).

ADDITIONAL WRITINGS ON SHAPEY
(Not cited in the catalogue)

Boehm, Yohanan. "Music," *The Jerusalem Post,* Monday, June 7, 1982.

Davis, Peter. "Pianos Still Stir Composers' Souls," *The New York Times,* Tuesday, June 7, 1981.

Gagne, Cole, and Tracy Caras. *Soundpieces: Interviews With American Composers.* Metuchen, NJ: Scarecrow Press, 1982.

Highwater, Jamake. "Ralph Shapey: Back Among the Dying," *Soho Weekly News* (New York), March 24, 1977.

Jacobson, Bernard. "The Enigma of Ralph Shapey," *Panorama - Chicago Daily News,* Sunday, May 10, 1969.

Laciar, Samuel L. "Shapey Conducts NYA Orchestra," *Philadelphia Evening Public Ledger,* Monday, November 28, 1939.

MacCardell, Charles. "Kennedy Center Friedheim Awards," *Musical America,* May 1991.

Mackelroy, Peter. "Army Relaxes to Let Soldier Conduct Concert At Dell Friday," *Philadelphia Record,* Wednesday, July 29, 1942.

Malitz, Nancy. "Shapey Celebrates A Big Decade," *Chicago Sun Times,* Tuesday, June 7, 1981.

McKay, J.R. "Report From Chicago: The Contemporary Chamber Players," *Current Musicology,* XV (1973), 15–16.

Nollan, James. "Mostly Serial, Mostly Academic," *American Record Guide,* July, 1964.

Page, Tim. "Concert: Elsa Charlston," *The New York Times,* Wednesday, December 1, 1982.

Reiter, James. "Villager to Conduct Orchestra at Labor Plaza," *Philadelphia, PA.,* Friday, July 25, 1947.

Ran, Shulamit. "An Angry Composer Forbids His Music To Be Performed," *The New York Times,* Sunday, May 8, 1977.

Rich, Alan. "Ralph Shapey at 60 - He Defies Neglect," *The New York Times,* Tuesday, May 10, 1981.

Rockwell, John. *All American Music: Composition in the Late Twentieth Century.* New York: Alfred Knopf, 1983.

Tommasini, Anthony. "A Craggy Personality Translates Into Sound," *The New York Times,* Sunday, May 5, 1996.

Uscher, Nancy. "Music for Strings By Ralph Shapey: A Survey," *American String Teacher,* Summer, 1984.

Valdes, Leslie. "Two Composers Share Top Friedheim Prize," *The Philadelphia Inquirer,* Tuesday, Oct. 30, 1990.

Von Rhein, John. "Paradise Almost Found: The City Grabs for the Big Time," *Chicago Tribune,* Wednesday, January 7, 1978.

Von Rhein, John. "Staying Composed," *Chicago Tribune,* Monday, April 9, 1989.

Webster, Daniel. "Speculum Musicae Honors Milton Babbitt," *The Philadelphia Inquirer,* Monday, February 26, 1991.

Willis, T. "A Composition About Composition in the Midwest," *Numus West* II/1 (1975), 13-15.

(No author given) "Four Composers Win Friedheim Awards," *Newsday* (New York), Monday, October 29, 1990.